Discover Your Enchanted Prosperity

How You Can Increase Your Financial Abundance, Success and Happiness — and Enjoy Your Spiritual Journey

(Text and Workbook)

from YourBodySoulandProsperity.com

Tom Marcoux

Executive Coach

Spoken Word Strategist

Speaker-Author of 32 books

CEO

A QuickBreakthrough Publishing Edition

Copyright © 2016 Tom Marcoux Media, LLC
ISBN: 0692638083
ISBN-13: 978-0692638088

All rights reserved. No part of this book may be reproduced or transmitted in any form by any means electronic or mechanical, including photocopying, recording or by any information storage and retrieval system without written permission from the publisher.

More copies are available from the publisher with the imprint QuickBreakthrough Publishing. For more information about this book contact: tomsupercoach@gmail.com

This book was developed and written with care. Names and details were modified to respect privacy.

Disclaimer: The author and publisher acknowledge that each person's situation is unique, and that readers have full responsibility to seek consultations with health, financial, spiritual and legal professionals. The author and publisher make no representations or warranties of any kind, and the author and publisher shall not be liable for any special, consequential or exemplary damages resulting, in whole or in part, from the reader's use of, or reliance upon, this material.:

Other Books by Tom Marcoux:
- Be Heard and Be Trusted: How to Get What You Want
- Emotion-Motion Life Hacks ... for More Success and Happiness
- Relax Your Way Networking
- Darkest Secrets of Persuasion and Seduction Masters
- Darkest Secrets of Charisma
- Darkest Secrets of Negotiation Masters
- Darkest Secrets of the Film and Television Industry Every Actor Should Know
- Darkest Secrets of Making a Pitch to the Film and Television Industry
- Darkest Secrets of Film Directing
- Now You See Me – Secrets of Power Networking – More Referrals

Praise for *Discover Your Enchanted Prosperity* and Tom Marcoux:

• "*Discover Your Enchanted Prosperity* is a rare combination of the spiritual and practical. You'll learn how to increase your financial abundance and to feel inner peace, too. Master Coach Tom Marcoux shows you how to take new action to expand your income and moments of happiness. Get this book!" – Dr. JoAnn Dahlkoetter, author, *Your Performing Edge* and Coach to CEOs and Olympic Gold Medalists

• "Tom Marcoux has distinguished himself as a coach, speaker and self-help author. His books combine his own philosophy and teachings, as well as those of other success experts, in a highly readable and relatable manner." – Danek S. Kaus, co-author of *Power Persuasion*

Praise for Tom Marcoux's Other Work:

• "Concerned about networking situations? Get *Relax Your Way Networking*. Success is built on high trust relationships. Master Coach Tom Marcoux reveals secrets to increase your influence." – Greg S. Reid, author, *Think and Grow Rich Series*

• "In Tom Marcoux's *Now You See Me*, the powerful and easy-to-use ideas can make a big difference in your business and your personal relationships." – Allen Klein, author of *You Can't Ruin My Day*

• "Marcoux's book *10 Seconds to Wealth* focuses on how each of us have divine gifts that we need to understand and use to be our best when the crucial '10 seconds' occur.... He identifies the divine gifts and shares how these gifts can help us create what we want in our lives, and the wealth we want." – Linda Finkle, author of *Finding The Fork In The Road: The Art of Maximizing the Potential of Business Partnerships*

• "In *Darkest Secrets of Persuasion and Seduction Masters: How to Protect Yourself and Turn the Power to Good*, learn useful countermeasures to protect you from being darkly manipulated."
– David Barron, co-author, *Power Persuasion*

• "In *Be Heard and Be Trusted*, Tom's advice on how to remain true to yourself and establish authentic rapport with clients is both insightful and reality based. He [shows how] to establish oneself as a credible expert."
- Arthur P. Ciaramicoli, Ed.D., Ph.D., author *The Curse of the Capable*

• "In *Reduce Clutter, Enlarge Your Life*, Marcoux will help you get rid of the physical and mental clutter occupying precious space in your life. You'll reclaim wasted energy, lower your stress, and find time for new opportunities." – Laura Stack, author of *Execution IS the Strategy*

Visit Tom's blog: www.BeHeardandBeTrusted.com

Tom Marcoux

CONTENTS*

Dedication and Acknowledgments	6
Empower Yourself in a Moment—Prosperity Plus Being Spiritual	11
Get In Motion–Stop Waiting for Motivation, Passion or 'The One Focus'	13
You Don't Need Willpower—You Need a System-for-Action	23
Create New Opportunities for You—Use the Power of the "AND-universe"	49
Create Your Brand and Clearly Communicate It	59
No More Hesitating!—Zero-in to Your Specific Focus and Niche Business	63
Ask for a Raise ... Get Money to Work for You	67, 89
What Will Change Your Life Forever?	99
Live Fearlessly	105
How You Can Cope When the Worst Happens	111
Final Word, Excerpt: *Darkest Secrets of Persuasion and Seduction Masters: How to Protect Yourself...*	135,136
About the Author; Special Offer to Readers of this Book	145,135

* This book includes even more material.

DEDICATION AND ACKNOWLEDGEMENTS

This book is dedicated to the terrific book and film consultant, and author Johanna E. Mac Leod. It is also dedicated to the other team members. Thanks to Barry Adamson II for editing some sections. Thanks to Johanna E. MacLeod for your insights and for rendering the front cover and back cover. Thanks to my father, Al Marcoux, for his concern and efforts for me. Thanks to my mother, Sumiyo Marcoux, a kind, generous soul. Thank you to Higher Power. Thanks to our readers, audiences, clients, my graduate/college students and my team members of Tom Marcoux Media, LLC.
The best to you.

Discover Your Enchanted Prosperity

"There's got to be a way to do business in which I feel more on purpose and I still enjoy my life!" my friend, Sherrie, said.

I agreed with her, and her comment inspired me to create one of my speech topics (and this book): *Discover Your Enchanted Prosperity.*

"When you enchant people, your goal [is] to fill them with great delight." – Guy Kawasaki

When I talk about Your Enchanted Prosperity, I'm referring to our uncovering that which delights us and other people. You discover how to serve people in ways that align with "what you're good at, what people will pay for and which clients you want."

I do not talk from theory. In my role as CEO of a company with team members in the United Kingdom, India and USA. I've learned to build High Trust Relationships.

As an Executive Coach, I help my clients take their lives to higher levels of success and happiness.

I've helped clients prepare to: lead a team, give sales presentations, do well in interviews, and build a brand.

My clients have taken a blog from zero to visitors from

173 countries, started businesses, and written a first book. Now, through this book, I serve as your Executive Coach. **This Book Helps You Leap Forward for More Success and Happiness:**

My work involves helping clients connect with their intuition. I use questions, and my clients experience this powerful process: **Insight—>Intuition—>Action.**

With this pattern, my clients have an experience of what I call *Catapult-Moments*. The catapult on an aircraft carrier kicks the plane forward fast. With Catapult-Moments, you jump forward. You find something new and better. You experience extraordinary progress. Clarity arrives and you feel so alive!

Part of this process helps you **develop skills, strength and stamina**—all vital elements for creating more success and happiness. I am truly happy to share with you insights and methods under the following headings:

- Discover Your Enchanted Prosperity
- Direct Ways to Increase Your Prosperity
- Protect and Build Your Energy

These sections are designed so you can connect with the material and quickly answer related questions.

I use certain phrases so people understand them and remember the ideas. For example, as I coach CEOs, business owners and others, I express my phrase: *"Take Command, Focus Your Brand."* Even if you don't have a business, you have a personal brand (it is what you're best known for). Your clarity makes it possible to get more of what you want in life.

Know that answering the provided questions even for just 20 seconds will give you a surprising advantage: You'll learn more about yourself and how to improve your daily actions.

You'll use strategies in achieving success for your life.
Let's take the next step.

Discover Your Enchanted Prosperity #1
Use the O.N.E. Process of Your Enchanted Prosperity

We use the O.N.E. process (as in "you're the one who knows in your heart"):

O – Open
N – Nurture intuition
E – Encourage

1. Open

Many people are closed in their thoughts. You hear their comments like "That won't work."

Instead, I suggest that we focus on "Let's find out!" Pick useful sources of information and encouragement. Many people (including "experts") talk from looking in the rearview mirror—that is, from history.

Instead, make plans and take action as you test things and find out.

Now it's your turn.

How can you devote some time and effort to be open to new possibilities? What good sources of inspiration and new ideas will you reach for?

2. Nurture intuition

Think of your intuition as a friend who will help when you make time and space to *listen* to intuition. We'd like intuition to inform us of the end game (steps 18, 19, 20) but intuition gives us Steps 1, 2, 3. When we complete Step 3, then intuition provides Steps 4, 5, 6.

To nurture your intuition, ask yourself, "Am I giving myself time to tinker and listen?" Frequently, in business, we do not have an immediate solution to a problem. If possible it helps to give ourselves some time (even one evening to "sleep on the problem"). Also talk with people and think through (or "tinker" with) the problem.

Now it's your turn.

How will you make space so you can listen to your intuition? Will you talk with other people and listen carefully to what YOU say and how your heart feels?

3. Encourage

To discover our Enchanted Prosperity path, we need to encourage ourselves. Do not wait for anyone's approval. Some people do not know how to give approval. Walt Disney did not wait for approval to make Disneyland. Steve Jobs did not wait for approval of all top music producers to offer songs at $0.99 each. In fact, the Beatles waited many long years before they finally made their songs available on iTunes.

As you do some experiments with projects, tell/ask yourself: "Good effort. Good action. What did I learn? Will I use this, refine it, or drop it?"

Additionally, it helps when your product/service encourages people to do new things and feel good as they do them. Steve Jobs insisted that iPod users needed to be able to get to their music in three clicks. Jobs led his team to make that possible. iPod users felt good in getting fast access to their music.

Now it's your turn.

What will you do to encourage yourself? How will you reward yourself for taking small steps forward?

To discover Your Enchanted Prosperity path, remember "Open, Nurture Intuition and Encourage." To build a brand is how you transform your current approach into Your Enchanted Prosperity. *For information on building your brand, see a 1.5 minute video – go to YouTube and type "Tom Marcoux Brand"*

How will you discover that which delights yourself and other people? How will you serve people in ways that align with "what you're good at, what people will pay for and which clients you want"?

Empower Yourself in a Moment— Prosperity Plus Being Spiritual

How can you shift to a spiritual place in yourself quickly? Two things: a) Breathe for Calmness and b) Shift to an *Empowered Second Thought*. (As a sidenote: A Chinese Proverb holds: "Man with unsmiling face must not open a shop." To bring a smile to your face and enhance your inner calm, use these two methods.).

a) Breathe for Calmness

Breathe deeply—in through your nose. Allow your belly to inflate. Hold your breath (perhaps say to yourself, "God relaxes me"). Breathe out and let your belly "deflate." This is called *belly breathing*. When you feel the need, do three to ten belly-breaths.

b) Shift to an *Empowered Second Thought*

Have you noticed times when you or someone near you has a first thought full of worry or fear? You can experience power and calmness by conditioning yourself to think an

Empowered Second Thought.

On the other hand, when we are fearful, our thoughts go to worry, survival and desperation. Desperate people do desperate things. However, a number of spiritual paths invite us to focus on love and shift away from fear.

We can do spiritual things born of spiritual ideas. I have a spiritual idea I have memorized as "KHH" or "K double H" – "kind, healthy, holy." Some people prefer to substitute "spiritual" for "holy." That works.

Do something kind, healthy and holy.

Can you approach increasing your prosperity by doing kind, healthy and holy actions? Yes!

- *Love your neighbor as yourself. – Jesus*
- *My religion is simple. My religion is kindness. – The Dalai Lama*
- *Be the change you wish to see in the world. - Gandhi*

Do you wish to see peace in the world? Then practice breathing for calmness and shifting to an *Empowered Second Thought*. One person who is calm affects those around her.

For over 14 years, I have taught a college level Comparative Religion course (I wrote the online course). Certain phrases from spiritual texts stay in my daily thoughts.

- *This is the day the Lord has made. Let us rejoice and be glad in it. – Psalm 118:24*
- *When you feel a peaceful joy, that's when you are near truth. – Rumi*
- *Being deeply loved by someone gives you strength, while loving someone deeply gives you courage. – Lao-tzu*
- *Thousands of candles can be lighted from a single candle, and the life of the candle will not be shortened. Happiness never decreases by being shared. – Buddha*

Can you do business in the manner of kindness and sharing light (value)? Yes!

[We can memorize spiritual quotes as an *Empowered Second Thought*.]

How will you approach your actions to increase your prosperity in the manner of kindness and sharing light (value)?

Discover Your Enchanted Prosperity #2

Get In Motion — Stop Waiting for Motivation, Passion or "The One Focus"

"I just don't feel passionate about anything enough," my friend Gerard said.

"I hear you. How about sticking that loaded word 'passion' into a drawer?" I replied.

"Just step toward things that you're curious about," I continued. "Don't buy into the myth that you must have peak-level motivation, passion or 'the One Focus.'"

The truth is: **You need to get in motion so your intuition can guide you.**

For a number of people, getting access to one's intuition can feel frustrating. Intuition will give you Steps 1,2,3 when you'd like to see the end game of Steps 18,19,20.

Still, when you get into motion, things become clearer.

"Climb the Mountain, See New Peaks"

I invite my clients to "Climb the Mountain" because without that motion, they won't know what is possible and they do NOT know what the next possibilities are.

For example, I was directing my second feature film when the father of one of the actors told me of a film-related association. On the association's website, I learned of a college teaching position. Within months, I was teaching at Cogswell Polytechnical College, and my career of teaching college students and graduate students had begun. I had no idea that I was to be a guest instructor two times at Stanford University. **What is important is to get in motion.**

Here's another example: "Are you sure that this book I'm doing will be a bestseller?" my client Alene asked.

How do I respond?—with the truth. I replied, "I don't know about this particular book. But I do know what this book will do for you. It will power-up your credibility. You can contact any podcast creator, radio show, TV show, blogger, and you can say, I'm Alene ____, and I'm the author of XY book."

More importantly, Alene will know that she *has* the material and a great understanding of her material. How? She just finished writing her book.

Remember the principle: "Climb the Mountain; See New Peaks." After she has the book and has been a guest on a podcast or blog, Alene starts seeing more possibilities. Having written a book on job searching, she might become a part-time instructor at a university, giving her another stream of income.

Here are two principles:
1. Be different; Be YOU.
2. Don't Compare; DO create.

1. Be different; Be YOU.

As I work with my clients, we see time and again that the person does *not* know ALL of which he or she is capable. It's like the person is at the bottom of that metaphorical mountain I'm talking about in this section.

If you asked me ten years ago, "Tom, will you write 32 books?" I'd reply: "No. That's not for me." Then, I wrote one book after another.

We only discover what we can do by doing something.

And you discover the real you by doing new things.

"In truth, I am a verb." – Steve Chandler

You are not what you did last year. You are NOT a label like "shy boy." No! You are a verb. What are you doing now? **Do the actions of a courageous person and you** *are* **courageous.**

When I talk with a prospective client for my unique version of executive coaching, I often say, "If you and I are a match .... If I'm your executive coach, *You Will Achieve More Than You Believe*. I know this to be a fact. When someone like me believes in you, you'll fill in the gaps.

I know how this works. I had three high school teachers:
- One taught me psychology: I earned a degree in psychology.
- One taught me English literature: I wrote 32 books, screenplays and directed feature films.
- The third taught me theology, and I wrote a college level Comparative Religion online course that I've been teaching for over 14 years.

These high school teachers saw more potential in me than I could imagine. When we work together, *You Will Achieve More Than You Believe."*

2. Don't Compare; DO create.

At one point, I had severe flu-like symptoms. I was in such pain that could not even read. The thought that arose for me was: *You're grateful for something? Do more with it.*

My point in sharing this idea "do more with it" is to encourage you to get out of the "compare with others" rut!

"If I can't be one of the best, I won't bother" is an approach a significant number of people have.

But that's NOT for you. We can't know how far we'll climb without getting into motion. **Create something. Try things on a small scale. Discover what you enjoy that you'll devote lots of time to study and conduct "experiments."** *You can't fail with an experiment.* I've experimented with running and yoga. I do a bit of yoga every day. That's a good start.

* * * * * *

Make Space to Be Creative in Many Ways

A powerful form of leverage is your easy access to creativity. How do you get that flowing? Express yourself in many ways and don't let fear slow you down.

For example, this morning, I woke up with a tune and some lyrics that arose in my dream. The lyrics were "You ain't nothing but a light show, baby."

I had no idea where that came from. Still, I got up, wrote down the lyrics, plugged in my keyboard and wrote down the notes.

I didn't know what this song would turn into. About forty minutes later, I discovered that the song fit a particular character in my first musical—that I have been writing off and on for two years.

My point is that when you express yourself and try

different forms of creativity—you don't know what new avenues will arise. For example, Post-it Notes arose from a failed attempt to develop a super-strong adhesive. Instead the creator of Post-it Notes had accidentally created a low-tack, reusable, pressure-sensitive adhesive.

We do not know where our creativity will lead. What's vital is that we get into motion.

How will you get into motion? How can you do some "experiments"?

_____

_____

_____

_____

_____

_____

_____

Discover Your Enchanted Prosperity #3

Use a "Miracle Moment" to Overcome Your Fear and Achieve Your Dream!

As I walked on the ocean floor, I took a deep breath and smiled. This was accomplishing one of my Big Dreams.

As a boy, I was thrilled by watching the Disney live-action feature film *20,000 Leagues Under the Sea*. I saw a team of men walking on the bottom of the ocean.

Later, I enjoyed James Cameron's film *The Abyss* which also included deep sea divers.

To get to the point of walking on the floor of the ocean, I had to *overcome two fears* related to *Sharks!* and to the claustrophobia of wearing a diving helmet.

Some days before my trip to the Grand Caymans, I practiced wearing a hood and visualizing that I was fine while wearing the helmet and walking on the ocean floor. *Positive visualization helped.*

I also asked about the presence of sharks, and I was informed that where I was diving sharks found the noise of various ships and the busy port to be off-putting.

Here's what I call the "Miracle Moment" to Really Achieve Your Dream:

It's the moment you connect with Something More Important than Your Fear.

Fulfilling my dream of walking on the ocean's floor was more important to me than my fear.

"Courage is not the absence of fear but rather the judgment that something is more important than fear." – Meg Cabot

Now it's your turn.
Write down your answers to these questions:

What is your Big Dream?

_____

_____

_____

What do you want to do?

_____

_____

What will *Feel Great!* to *you* as you're accomplishing your Big Dream?

_____

_____

_____

_____

What will you be able to do that you cannot do now— when you accomplish your Big Dream?

_____

_____

_____

What fears are connected to what you need to do to accomplish your Big Dream?

_____

_____

_____

What about your Big Dream is More Important than Your Fear?

_____

The above process is connected to what you want *to feel* when you're realizing your dream.

As an Executive Coach, I often help clients move beyond their comfort zone and to accomplish extraordinary things. I help my clients connect with *Big Energy* (which is heartfelt) and then they have something More Important than their fear.

Take the time to really connect with what moves your heart. Then, from this foundation, spring up and make progress to accomplish your dream.

**Special Section for those people having trouble choosing a dream.

For those who have a difficulty in allowing themselves "to dream" I have a process: "Convert a *Big No!* into a *Big Want!*"

For many of us it is easy to name what we do NOT like about our current life.

Here is the pattern:

Big No!	Big Want!
1. I do NOT want _____	1a. I want _____ instead.
2. I want _____ to STOP.	2a. I want _____ to *replace* that which bothers me.
3. I DISLIKE _____ in my life.	3a. I would like to have (or do) _____.

So the above items in the box show the pattern you can use to convert a Big No! into Big Want!

Discover Your Enchanted Prosperity #4

You Don't Need Willpower—You Need a System-for-Action

"I have good willpower for what I eat for breakfast, but if I'm awake at 11 pm, I'll eat ice cream," Anne, an audience member said.

Willpower may fail us.

Here's what is better: a *System-for-Action.*

The idea is to **make a decision once and then have momentum carry you forward.**

With a number of clients, I bring in the below form (that I created) titled the *SEE and SEE NEXT Grid.*

First, I'll describe the "Yes! Energy" approach. Yes! Energy relates to a celebration of life and good possibilities.

This is unusual. Why? Because often when people talk about their current situation they fall into complaining. They're basically describing all the things that they dislike, and they want to say NO! to them. We hear comments like: "I'm not getting paid enough for this" or "I hate going to work with those people."

On the other hand, *Yes! Energy* celebrates the blessings

you already have in life. Such Yes! Energy is attractive to more opportunities.

Now let's view the valuable elements of the *SEE and SEE NEXT Grid*:

SEE – with Yes! Energy	SEE NEXT – with Yes! Energy
Where are you now?	What's next? (general brainstorming)
How far have you come?	Level 1 – Goals "Good"
What did you learn?	Level 2 – Goals "Excellent"
How can you do things better?	Level 3 – Goals "AMAZING!"
What do you SEE now that you did *not* see before?	3 Goal Types #1: Golden Pull Goals
What's working?	3 Goal Types #2: Dark Boot Goals
What's *not* working?	3 Goal Types #3: Green Tranquility Goals
What do you want to STOP (in your life)?	"What you dread gets you ahead."
What are you grateful for?	Marketing: "Always have something to invite people to."
What are you excited about?	Make it so "I enjoy enrolling people"
What can you praise yourself for?	"3 Prong Approach" (to avoid scattering your energy)
What can you reward yourself for? (What will be these rewards?)	You need to test/take action in the real world. (*"Failure is the test of greatness."* – Herman Melville) You take action and then adjust as you go along. You cannot get by on just reading. Here we work well in handling fear.
Other Comments Fit Here:	What do you need to learn?
	What do you need to let go?

	(What's NOT working?)
	Where's the FUN?

	4 Questions for Niche Business:
	    a) Who do you want to help?
	    b) Where's the fun?
	    c) How is your target market like (similar) you?
	    d) How do you heal them and a part of you?

	"Set the Games" – "Keep Score and Achieve More" – Put Systems in Place

The *SEE and SEE NEXT Grid* helps my clients set up a System-for-Action.

Often, I use this form in the middle of a scheduled year of coaching. It helps to see where you are and how far you have come.

Below I'll now give you the opportunity to fill in answers to the questions found in the *SEE and SEE NEXT Grid*. Many of the questions are self-evident. At times when more description is needed, I augment the questions.

We begin with the "See" section which helps you identify your current situation. (This is where you "See" where you are.)

Where are you now?

_____

How far have you come?

_____

What did you learn?

How can you do things better?

What do you SEE now that you did *not* see before?

What's working?

What's *not* working?

What do you want to STOP (in your life)?

What are you grateful for?

What are you excited about?

What can you praise yourself for?

___

What can you reward yourself for? (What will be these rewards?)

___

We now move onto the SEE NEXT section. On the form I include the idea "with Yes! Energy." By this I mean you'll do better by connecting with your positive energy as you do this process. Imagine taking the energy of doubt or fear and placing it into a metaphorical drawer.

Take doubt and fear off center stage. Give yourself a break and a mini-vacation from fear pushing you around.

Just do this process with a "let's take a look at this" approach.

What's next? (general ... brainstorming)

It helps to avoid holding back. Just write down some things you want next—and do not pause to think about *how* you might accomplish them. Use this chance to do some brainstorming.

___

___

Level 1 – Goals "Good"
Level 2 – Goals "Excellent"
Level 3 – Goals "AMAZING!"

We often hear about people giving up on their New Years

Resolutions. Why? Many of them are *not* skillful in setting their goals. Set a goal too high and it might give you too much fear and cause procrastination. Set a goal too low and you have *no* excitement or energy for the goal.

The solution is to set **3 Levels of Goals:**
a. Good
b. Excellent
c. *Amazing!*

For an author, the goals might be:
In a month:
a. Sell 30 copies of one's book (Good)
b. Sell 300 (Excellent)
c. Sell 3,000 *(Amazing!)*

When we think of *Amazing!*, we get excited. We also need to think on a *whole new level*. How can you sell 3,000 copies? — you cannot do it alone. You need help. For example, authors often team up with other authors. When one author has book about to debut, the other authors promote the book to their own esubscriber lists.
Goals "Good"

Goals "Excellent"

Goals "AMAZING!"

---

3 Goal Types #1: Golden Pull Goals
3 Goal Types #2: Dark Boot Goals
3 Goal Types #3: Green Tranquility Goals

Golden Pull Goals are the fun goals to talk about. They comprise the goals that *pull us forward*. We consider them our heartfelt dreams.

The truth I've seen is that many of us will only do certain tasks to *avoid pain*. I call these tasks/goals: **Dark Boot Goals.** It's like having a big boot kicking you in the rear. The pain only stops when you take appropriate action.

For example, a number of people I've talked with tell me that they only do tax paperwork to avoid tax penalties. Their efforts relate to the Dark Boot Goal of getting one's tax return done and turned in.

I've learned, after accomplishing many things, directing feature films, writing 32 books and more, that only accomplishing projects does *not* yield a happy life. So I added what I call **Green Tranquility Goals.** These are things you do that support your well-being.

My clients have written these goals:

Golden Pull Goals: write a book, direct a feature film, move to New York and get a new job

Dark Boot Goals: complete taxes paperwork, exercise daily and let go of excess weight

Green Tranquility Goals: meditate for 5 minutes in the morning, walk near trees, read a novel in a hot bath.

Golden Pull Goals

Dark Boot Goals

Green Tranquility Goals

"What you dread gets you ahead."

It seems to be a paradox in the universe that what you do *not* like doing in this moment is that which can serve as a *springboard for more success*.

Often, when I give a speech, I mention: "There are some

people in this room who would do well to update their resumes. But you dread it, right? I'm right there with you. Still, I've learned: *What you dread gets you ahead."*

So now admit (and write down) something that you dread but you know will actually position you for more success and happiness.

Marketing: "Always have something to invite people to."

What can you invite people to? A free conference call can serve well. First, the prospective customers do not need to spend money or travel anywhere. You can post the recording of the call so those who miss the call can hear the material at a later date.

Make it so "I enjoy enrolling people"

If you keep telling the tired and disempowering story that "you don't like marketing or selling" then you keep getting that experience. Instead, tell yourself: "I'm learning ways so *I enjoy enrolling people."*

With clients, I guide them through questions like:
- "Do you like what you do?"
- "Do you enjoy talking about what you do?"
- "Do you know for certain that you help people?"
- "Do you feel good when you help people get the benefits of what you do?"

The truth is: a number of people dislike talking about money and the required fee. **Use this method called "the sandwich."** The bottom piece of bread is asking questions and helping the person experience the VALUE of what you're offering. In the middle of the "sandwich" talk about the fee. Make sure to avoid ending any conversation with just talking about the fee. Instead, make sure that the topside "piece of bread" is about *VALUE and enjoyment for the client.* Rehearse until you're more and more comfortable with your sales conversations. **Find ways to enjoy enrolling people.**

"3-Pronged Approach" (to avoid scattering your energy)

A number of business owners I know tell me that they feel overwhelmed in that they're doing too many different things to market their products/services. A real problem surfaces with that pattern: One fails to put enough effort into any one marketing modality. It's better to pick three vital ways to do marketing. Hence the phrase "3 Pronged Approach."

You avoid scattering your energy and focus. Further, if any two marketing modes are disappointing in the current moment, you have another one that can work. This goes along with the pattern that I shared in my book *Darkest Secrets of Making a Pitch for Film and Television: How You Can Get a Studio Executive, Producer, Name Actor or Investor to Say Yes to Your Project.*

In that book, I talked about how a screenwriter can feel empowered with a *3-Pronged Approach*: "Have one screenplay in the marketplace, one that you're finishing and one that you're starting."

Similarly, have three marketing modes that you pursue with great focus and energy.

One of my clients 1) goes to Toastmasters events, 2) attends Meetup events of entrepreneurs and 3) writes a well-received blog. She can modify or adapt her 3-Pronged Approach while she monitors her results from her first "marketing campaign."

You need to test/take action in the real world. ("Failure is the test of greatness." – Herman Melville) You take action and then adjust as you go along. You cannot get by on just reading. Here we work well in handling fear.

Fear can shut you down. *The plan here is to face it.* That means you need to step into the real world and try things out. Some of them won't work so you might say that some actions might "fail." That is okay. It helps to test ideas out without putting down too much money—if possible. I'll try a new title for a book by writing a blog article on that topic and title. Then I see how many people share the particular article.

Handling fear is also about simply acknowledging that it is present—and you still go out and get in front of potential customers. Yes, you'll make mistakes. But you won't know what really works until you stop reading and start doing.

Years ago, I had a particular friend who read a lot and talked a lot, but did not complete a product and bring it to the marketplace. It's sad really.

Thus, it's important to rehearse your presentation and then go out and connect with potential customers.

What do you need to learn?

What do you need to let go? (What's NOT working?)

Where's the fun?

4 Questions for Niche Business:
a) **Who do you want to help?**
b) **Where's the fun?**
c) **How is your target market similar to you?**
d) **How do you heal them and a part of you?**

These four questions can yield an invigorating target for your efforts. I worked with a client and the "combined answer" that the four questions inspired was: "Teach women at a conference in Hawaii."

"Set the Games"—"Keep Score and Achieve More"— Put Systems in Place

Earlier I spoke of "You need to test/take action in the real world." I help clients who own businesses to **"See the**

Three" which looks like this:

This week:

a) How many sales conversations have you had?

b) How many referrals did you ask for?

c) How many times did you ask someone to buy something?

The important thing is to "set up a game." With the "See the Three" questions above you can measure your progress. In this case, "the game" is to do better than your previous score (from the previous week).

I coined this phrase: "Keep Score and Achieve More."

It works. Use a Progress Log.

You can even get yourself to go to bed earlier. One of my clients set up a game: "Turn off the TV close to 10 pm." The first night she turned off the TV at 12:10 AM. The next night was at 11:30 PM. She kept getting better at her new "game."

Some people protest and say, "Life is not a game." We acknowledge the truth that life includes serious experiences. Still, we understand that game-play energizes people.

Years ago, I wrote about what I called "The Video Games Theory." The idea was that people become addicted to games because a) they can get better at them, b) instant gratification arrives in a constant tally of one's score, and c) one gets a fun break from the real world.

Author Zig Ziglar wrote about how no one would go bowling if they could not see the pins drop. This relates to my phrase "Keep Score and Achieve More."

Be sure to identify the most important measurements. Earlier, I mentioned "See the Three."

When I say, "Put Systems in Place," I mean that human beings do much based on setting good habits. When you have a system in place you do not have to suffer through pushing yourself to do a particular behavior. A system makes the behavior automatic. Author Steve Chandler advised one of his clients to write up an invoice immediately after any client session. In this way, Steve's client had a system and he stopped procrastinating on writing up and sending out invoices.

Here's another example of a System:

Monday – devote one hour to identify 17 phone numbers of prospective clients to call

Tuesday – devote 1.5 hours to call the 17 phone numbers.

Now it's your turn. Write down some form of measurement you can use. "Keep Score and Achieve More."

_____

_____

_____

A number of my clients find it helpful to type up their answers to the various questions of the *SEE and SEE NEXT Grid* so they have a clear plan for their next actions.

Tom Marcoux

Discover Your Enchanted Prosperity #5

How Your Enchanted Prosperity Works

"I want my business to feel magical—like when I first had the idea," my client Kara said.

I agree and that is part of the essence of *Discover Your Enchanted Prosperity*.

Let's face this:

You want magic.

Let's talk about magic as relating to *Joy, Excitement, and Delight.*

Delight relates to something extra and surprising.

For the elements of Your Enchanted Prosperity let's consider the metaphor of a "magical pin." Disneyland has many pins. In fact, after I saw the film *Tomorrowland*, I had the idea that it would be fun to buy a *Tomorrowland* (film-related) pin while I was IN Tomorrowland. Yes, I got my pin (during Disneyland's 60th Anniversary) while I was in Southern California. I went to the theme park after giving a seminar in North Hollywood.

We'll use the P.I.N. process:

P – pray
I – inhale
N – non-judge

1. Pray

"If the only prayer you ever say in your entire life is thank you, it will be enough."– Meister Eckhart

Prayer can be part of using affirmations.

Some people report that affirmations do not work for them. We can understand that saying "I am thin" while looking at one's body that's 60 pounds overweight is counterproductive. Part of one's mind says fervently, "You're lying. That's not true."

I find a difficulty with the "I am thin" affirmation because it's describing a proposed "Future State" (as in state of being).

Instead, you can change your affirmation into an *Action-Affirmation* of "I eat like a thin person." Then you can turn it into a prayer with "[God, Higher Power] helps me eat like a thin person." [My friend Moonwater talks about a "Pattern-Affirmation," and she is emphasizing a pattern of behavior.]

Here's another example: "God blesses me as I ask for referrals."

You can add to a prayer: "This or better." You can also add "For my good and the good of all involved."

This all applies to Your Enchanted Prosperity when you turn your prayers into something like: "God help me serve my clients better. Please inspire me with better ideas."

2. Inhale (breathing)

How do you know that you're doing fine?

I just took in a deep breath. I find that deep breathing energizes me when necessary. Also deep breathing is helpful for calming down.

Let's talk about deep breathing or "belly breathing."

Go through these steps: Breathe in through your nose and allow your belly area to expand. Hold you breath for a moment. Then breathe out and allow your belly area to deflate. Practice this multiple times. With your added calmness, you have the energy to be friendly to people. This will add to your ability to expand Your Enchanted Prosperity.

One Chinese proverb holds: "Man with unsmiling face should not open a shop." We can add to this Man and Woman who practice belly breathing naturally smile more!

3. Non-judge (let go)

Judgment places restrictions on happiness. Judgment says, "If it doesn't go the way I want it to then people are wrong and things are wrong."

On the other hand, *non-judgment* has preferences instead of demands.

People often resist when we demand something. Instead, we can hold preferences. An author I know, Lydia, wants her book to be a bestseller. Still, using non-judgment, Lydia holds to the *preference* of having a bestseller. If the book sells 5,000 copies (missing the best-seller status), she lets go of a judgment that "she should have worked harder and because of that she failed."

The late author Richard Carlson told me some years ago that his bestselling book *Don't Sweat the Small Stuff* was his tenth book. His other books had no where the readership of his bestselling, tenth book. Still he did not stay in the judgment that he was unsuccessful as a writer. He loved to write and he kept moving forward with writing.

Here's where Your Enchanted Prosperity fits in. Find

what you're good at, what people will pay for and what clients you want. Take a breath and realize that the universe will guide the timing of when the blessings roll in.

Practice non-judgment. Enjoy the blessings you do have.

Your Enchanted Prosperity blossoms from aligning yourself with what is good in you and in the universe.

Where does Your Enchanted Prosperity Start?
The cars collided with a heartrending crash! Oscar winner F. Murray Abraham survived a car accident. He wondered, "Why had I been spared?" He fell into despair. Then he connected with Higher Power and realized: "I was spared to act!"

What is it that YOU are here to do?
Every day I write (32 books so far) and I rehearse for my next speech. Make your new year great—loving and creative. *Express what YOU are here to do.*

A number of people lament: "I have not found my passion yet!"

I reply, "Look around for something that sparks your interest." If you don't know what your passion is—try a "theme." Some themes can be:
- something to do with writing
- something that helps animals
- something related to taking photos

Here's an idea: "You can't fail with an experiment." That is, you try something and see what you learn.

What experiments will you try that may support Your Enchanted Prosperity?

Discover Your Enchanted Prosperity #6

Release Yourself from Limits Placed By Old Rigid Thoughts on Money

"We can't afford that," Serena's parents said over and over. Unfortunately, she swallowed that idea just like the chicken soup her mother made for her.

When I give a speech on "Discover Your Enchanted Prosperity," I find that I need to carefully guide the audience to different starting points than tired, restrictive ideas.

Such ideas include: "We can't afford that"; "Money doesn't grow on trees," and "You have to work hard." We'll use the O.W.N. process. (We're looking at the process to OWN your thoughts and empower yourself.)

O – open
W – work it through
N – nurture yourself

1. Open
Psychologists refer to *confirmation bias* which is defined as "a phenomenon wherein decision makers have been shown to actively seek out and assign more weight to evidence that

confirms their hypothesis, and ignore or underweigh evidence that could disconfirm their hypothesis (sciencedaily.com)."

The big problem with confirmation bias is that no new information can get in. In essence, one only pays attention to details that support the beliefs one *already holds*.

I invite you to pay close attention to your automatic thoughts and comments. Challenge yourself to see if you're allowing confirmation bias to keep out new ideas.

Don't be trapped by dogma—which is living with the results of other people's thinking. Don't let the noise of others' opinions drown out your own inner voice. – Steve Jobs

Instead, seek to open your eyes to possibilities and learning from your own new experiences.

2. Work it through

The old restrictive idea that people say that they "can't afford something," is often *not* true!

Do you *really* want something? Have you surprised yourself in how you somehow got it?

I wanted to walk on the ocean floor, and I made sure to have the funds to make that dream happen.

Instead of defaulting to "we can't afford," change your language. Say something like: "My funds are going a different direction at the moment."

I've talked with people who would like to write a book or become a professional speaker. But they have some old rigid thoughts about what it means to be "an expert."

For example, on Facebook, one of my colleagues in a group for professional speakers posted this question: "Can I get some feedback on this? To be a motivational speaker you have to be an industry professional or people won't listen to you."

I replied, "Years ago, I read something that Bob Bly wrote. From his inspiration I distilled the idea down to **"An expert is someone who has a system that people like and use."** My point is that in today's rapid-moving life, one cannot know everything on a topic (That's part of why I read 74 books last year.) Still, one needs to speak with authority (evidence, experience, authenticity). The best to you"

Now I want to address "evidence, experience, authenticity." I usually refer to this as "A double E—as in A.E.E." **Unfortunately, too many of us simply buy into tired, old rigid ideas about how one can earn money.**

A number of people have accomplished great things without earning a college degree—including Steve Jobs, Henry Ford, Bill Gates, Lady Gaga, Frank Lloyd Wright, Buckminster Fuller, Mark Zuckerberg, and James Cameron.

I want to add that letting go of limited thinking is helpful. For example, author Jeanna Gabellini posted on Facebook 12/24/15: "What's the biggest amount of money you can imagine having at once?"

I replied: "$4 billion—when my franchises (*Jack AngelSword, Jenalee Storm, TimePulse, Crystal Pegasus*) all sell. [My imagination is a good friend.]"

Jeanna replied: "Seeing it in your mind is what generates the reality...so you're right on target!"

My questions to you are: Are you ready to drop limiting beliefs? Can you imagine big things for your adventure of life?

3. Nurture yourself

To push back against the old restrictive thoughts on money, you need REAL energy and a new focus. This reminds me of how my sweetheart taught me the value of an occasional headache medication. She told me, **"When you're** in pain, you're *losing* energy."

So I dropped my old idea to never take headache medication.

Let's go further:

Old rigid thoughts on money are stealing your energy!

As a CEO and as an Executive Coach, there are times when I offer ideas—and I'm helping the person access her own intuition. I say, "The ideas are a buffet table. Take what you like—leave the rest."

Here's my next idea for you:

Let Go of the Thought, "Only By Hard Work Does Money Arrive"

"We'll take a family vacation to Disneyland," my father said, when he received a payment from an insurance company to cover the damage a delivery truck inflicted on his car. I was in middle of a tough time at work and I could not get away. So I said, "How about you put that money into a CD (Certificate of deposit account)—and save it? We can go on the trip after I complete this project at work."

My father did NOT save the money. It just slipped through his fingers. My family never went on that vacation.

This further reinforced in me the importance of **"Use effective thought in money matters."**

The truth I've discovered is: **"Money arrives by effective thought."** Other effective thoughts include: a) saving money is a valuable discipline, b) watching your budget is crucial and c) study and make space to think of creative ideas. **Ideas can be a source of income creation.**

How will you make space for thinking of useful IDEAS?

Discover Your Enchanted Prosperity #7

Find the Magic of Your Enchanted Prosperity— and Uplift Your Business Model

"I didn't know I'd be afraid so much of the time before I started my business," my client Amy said, at the beginning of our work together.

"I hear you. The idea is not about never feeling fear. The idea is just NOT to stay there," I said.

I put two ideas together:
- Replace worry with action.
- Fill your mind with something other than fear.

To fill your mind with something other than fear, it's important to connect with "the Magic of Your Enchanted Prosperity." The idea is to expand your thinking and feeling.

We begin with this quote:

"To feel the love of people whom we love is a fire that feeds our life. But to feel the affection that comes from those whom we do not know....widens out the boundaries of our being, and unites all living things." – Pablo Neruda (poet)

He was talking about how his work was appreciated by a number of people whom he did not know personally.

Still, I see how the idea of "widens out the boundaries of our being" applies to Your Enchanted Prosperity.

Years ago, I had a particular friend who called any day "ruined" if he "did *not* have a good workout." As he complained bitterly, I was reminded of an old phrase: "The canvas is too small."

The opposite of a *too small canvas* is "united with all living things." You can connect with that which spiritual and comforting: **We are connected with Higher Power and with each other.**

Such a spiritual idea is a foundational point of Your Enchanted Prosperity.

You're *not* only doing business efforts for your own wealth. You are engaged in living on the level of compassion and contribution to the forward movement of humankind.

I personally focus on this with the mission of my own company:

We create energizing, encouraging edutainment for our good and humankind's rise. – Tom Marcoux Media, LLC Mission

One example of wide boundaries and united *with all living things* is the approach of Anita Roddick, founder of The Body Shop. At the beginning, Roddick provided reusable containers in efforts to reduce waste. Roddick also devoted efforts to provide a fair price for natural ingredients or handcrafts her company purchased from people in what were called "often marginalized countries."

Back to my friend (some time ago) who spoke of his obsession with his own body. He once said to me, "I had energy in the 80's. Where did it go?"

During the conversation, I said: "In the '80s you were part of a team wanting to do good things and serve people. How are things going now? Have you found someone new to serve?"

Silence.

Eventually, that friend drifted away from my life.

"I am attracted to love, joy and excellence in people."
– Jack Canfield, co-founder of the Chicken Soup for the Soul series

This section is about uplifting your business model. How can you make your work connected to love, joy and excellence?

"The hardest thing is to find your genuine self – because that is what people want. You will be a success when you find that."
– Bobby McFerrin (winner of 10 Grammy Awards)

So making your business work on a higher level is connected to authenticity and contribution to humankind.

How can you serve people and help them do better in life? How can you focus on love, joy and excellence in terms of your business model? What excites you? How can you invest what you love *into* your work?

_____

_____

_____

_____

Discover Your Enchanted Prosperity #8

Create New Opportunities for You – Use the Power of the "AND-universe"

"I really want to increase my income, but I feel like something is holding me back. Something inside me," my friend Sean said.

"Let me share with you the idea of *'This is an AND-universe.'* In this case, I'm talking about how you can be full of gratitude AND 'go for more,'" I replied.

When I speak on *Discover Your Enchanted Prosperity*, I often work with people who are stuck because they were shut down by limiting beliefs in childhood. They heard comments like "just be grateful for what you have and don't be greedy."

Such a concept can function as **chains** on one's energy, viewpoint and fulfillment of personal potential. How? Many of us do not want to be "bad" or "greedy." That's understandable. Still, **I know people who have devoted themselves to serving customers *and* they have earned a terrific, prosperous way of life.** Did you see the powerful word? It's **"AND."**

Many of us notice that there is a "gap" between where we are now and where we want to be. But it is folly to say, "I'll only be happy when XY happens." **So the better plan is to enjoy this moment AND "go for more."** You'll find that you can even *enjoy* the process of finding out how you can serve more people in different ways.

We'll use the G.A.P. process:

G – gratitude

A – action

P – preparation

1. Gratitude

Gratitude is a strong stance. When I was trained in karate moves, the instructors guided me to have a strong stance. Such a stance provided support so one could kick. Still, such a stance was *flexible* so you could move in any direction

Gratitude fills us with positive energy. We can shift to gratitude and step out of a mood of disappointment or even a mood of worry.

To begin the shift, write on a sheet of paper (or in a personal journal), **"I am grateful for . . ."** Now note 10 things that you appreciate in your life.

Many years ago, I worked as part of tech-group inside a top bank. This position did *not* employ my best talents. Still, every morning, I recited my *10 Blessings* as I took a shower. I'd say, "I'm grateful for my sweetheart, my excellent health, my friends, the financial abundance of my job ..."

This practice helped me enjoy my present moment AND energized me to even work on my own company after returning from the bank each day.

Numerous authors have noted the value of starting from gratitude. **The universe sends more opportunities to you — and you have MORE to be grateful for.**

2. Action

One of my favorite quotes is:

"Replace worry with action." – Steve Chandler

Have you noticed that worried people get stuck? And some miserable people truly spread misery! Instead, we have two ways to develop more and better in our lives.

1) Shift to an outlook of gratitude

2) Take action.

"Actions seems to follow feeling, but really actions and feeling go together; and by regulating the action, which is under the more direct control of the will, we can indirectly regulate the feeling."

– William James

I've noted that when I implement "Replace worry with action," **I simply feel better.**

All I need to do is a simple action. It can be just listing the next people for me to call. I make a couple of phone calls and I feel much better.

Now it's your turn. What small simple actions can you take to get yourself moving in a positive direction?

3. Preparation

I have coached thousands of people (clients and audiences) with this phrase: "Courage is easier when I'm prepared."

By this I mean, that my preparation quiets down my fear and I take action to improve my circumstances.

I'll add this phrase:

The Answer to Fear is Rehearsal.

In college, I had to direct a final project: a live television show. I was afraid. I went to a senior and asked for advice. Paul said, "Don't bury your head in your script. Watch your monitors."

So I went back to my dorm room and drew five "TV

Monitors" on five separate sheets of paper. I taped them to the wall. I rehearsed by glancing at the script and then up at the monitors.

When I directed that live television show, I was glad I had rehearsed.

While Camera One was "live"—the background painting visible on Camera Two fell down.

Calmly, I had the crew fix the background during a commercial break.

Rehearsal had saved the day [at least the project and my grade].

Recently, I was invited to give a brief speech. Two weeks later, I stepped on stage and I did well. I know that my 15 rehearsal sessions helped! (Yes, I keep a *Progress Log* of my rehearsals. ... By the way, you can rehearse a section during a phone call with a friend. I often rehearse in a car while a team member drives.

Now it's your turn. What form of preparation or rehearsal can help you do better when you're in a pressure-filled moment? How will you schedule some rehearsal?

As an Executive Coach, I help new business owners and seasoned professionals free themselves from the chains of limited thinking and lack of consistent action.

When I talk about *Discover Your Enchanted Prosperity*, I inspire the audience to realize that this is an "AND-universe." **You can enjoy the moment as you focus on gratitude AND you can "go for more."**

How will you approach each day with BOTH gratitude and taking action to create new and better in your life?

Discover Your Enchanted Prosperity #9

Heal Up—"Wealth Up!"

"I don't understand. I do well for a time and then I fall back into self-sabotaging habits," my friend Andrea said.

"I hear you," I replied. "For many of us, we apply some techniques but it's only a temporary, cosmetic change. What really helps is to develop an attitude that I call 'Healthy Humility.'"

Healthy Humility is a realistic approach that acknowledges that our perception, in a particular moment, can be off. We approach each day keeping our eyes open for new opportunities to learn.

For example, one time I traveled some cities over and visited my parents.

In recent years, I've seen my father become quite bitter.

This particular day, my father launched into some mean, loud comments.

I saw my mother's face collapse in a frown. She had been living with my father's increasing bitterness in his elderly years.

I patted my mother gently on the arm and I said, "I'm *not*

going to stand up." By remaining seated, I used something that *my healthy humility had uncovered.* In the past, my standing up would lead to my refuting my father's mean words with my own loud voice. Standing up was part of a pattern of speeding up my own heart and getting it racing. That would merely escalate the situation.

Instead, from a seated position, I maintained my calm. I had learned to keep myself calm.

My point in sharing this example is to show *the value of healthy humility and learning from each situation.* I'm looking for ways in which I can act more effectively. I'm looking to use healthy humility to find my own mistakes and areas to improve.

You see, invoking some quick-fix application of some trendy technique for prosperity often does not work in the long run.

Now, I invite you to *use healthy humility so you can unleash a great flow of prosperity in your life*

The experience of prosperity is *not* just about bringing a lot of money into your life. It's also about saving money and making good, supportive decisions about money and budgets.

If we're having a roller-coaster ride with prosperity going up and down in our lives, it's likely that **we need to "Heal Up" some subconscious patterns and patterns-of-self-sabotage.** We'll use the H.E.A.L. process:

H - hear
E - experience
A - adapt
L – learn

1. Hear

Some people simply don't hear or listen to the life lessons as they arrive. Do you know some people who never admit their mistakes?

"Do you trust someone who never admits a mistake?" I asked college students in one of my classes.

"No!" they replied.

Let's make this practical for you: **So if you were to listen to your current life lessons, what would they be?**

Maria, one of my clients, said, "I'd get more sleep!"

Jerry, a friend, said, "I'd make appointments with myself to make prospecting phone calls five days a week."

Now it's your turn.

What is *not* working for you? What new actions would help you do better? If this "chapter of your life" has two life lessons for you—what are they? How can you make your life better?

2. Experience

Have you noticed that some people are so closed-down that they apparently do not fully experience a life lesson? The result is: They keep repeating the pattern over and over again.

I've also observed that some people do not let another person's pain in. By this, I mean that they fail to empathize with the other person's pain and personal situation.

When you're able to experience the world from another person's point of view, you're well on your way to be a compassionate person.

Using compassion can help you do better with your own business, for example. You can think ahead to what the customers need and prefer. You can create customer loyalty.

Now, it's your turn.

Are you making space to experience the "bad news"? Can you feel another person's (a customer, co-worker, employee) pain? Can you make space to be compassionate and then do something to make the situation better?

3. Adapt

Ultimately, when you keep your healthy humility functioning well, you can *adapt more readily* to tough situations. How? First, you're alert to things. Secondly, you can effectively use the energy that would have been lost in hiding or covering up reality.

Now, it's your turn.

What needs to be better in your life? How can you adapt to the situation? What new decisions and actions do you need to implement?

4. Learn

Learn where your weakness points are. I used to buy way more books than I do today. When I got rid of 243 boxes of stuff (see my book *Reduce Clutter, Enlarge Your Life*), many of those boxes were filled with books.

So I've learned to be more selective in my book purchases.

In fact, in 2015, I let go of 341 books. (My sweetheart is relieved that those books were "banished" from our home. I'm grateful for her patience.)

Now, it's your turn.

What do you need to learn? How can you make space so you can heal in some ways? Do you need to change how you interact with family, customers or supervisors?

Is it time to consider working with a counselor, coach and or therapist? (Some difficulties require that we get help. It takes courage to ask for help and take efforts to improve one's life. It is worth it!)

As an Executive Coach, I find that clients, at times, need to go deeper. It's not just about adding techniques. Often, one needs to heal and clear the debris of past pain and past mistakes. When I speak on *Discover Your Enchanted Prosperity*, I share how we can heal and rise up to higher levels of success and happiness.

If you find that your prosperity seesaws between up and down, you may need to devote some effort to the H.E.A.L. process.

H - hear
E - experience
A - adapt
L – learn

What can you learn so you provide more value to the marketplace?

_____

_____

_____

_____

_____

_____

_____

_____

Direct Way to Increase Your Prosperity #1

Create Your Brand and Clearly Communicate It

"2 Seconds.

2 seconds is a time duration that means a lot to me.

In 2 seconds, years ago, I was a stuntman, holding onto the hood of a classic, cherry-red, 50s Chevy truck—going 63 miles an hour. Holding on by my fingertips.

In 2 seconds, I saved the life of a little boy.

And in 2 seconds, I can share an idea with you that can make an impact. You can use this moment as a pivot point. *So you can raise your life to higher levels of success and happiness,*" I said, opening one of my speeches.

"The idea I want to share with you is *Emotion-Motion Life Hacks*. A Life Hack is a technique that improves your productivity and efficiency. But an Emotion-Motion Life Hack helps you use the Emotion-component. You make a decision ONCE and you get carried by momentum."

I share the above opening of one of my speeches to illustrate that you need to be compelling at the beginning of a speech. The benefit *"you can raise your life to higher levels of success and happiness"* is expressed in the beginning of the speech.

We need to remember that our brand is about how the other *person experiences benefits*. It's **not** about *the how* of our process of delivering the product/service.

Now, we'll use a formula I developed for my clients and audiences:

Tom Marcoux's Branding Formula:
I help people   _____
to achieve   _____
They feel   _____
My clients say   _____

Here's another way to view this:
I help people __(verb)__
to achieve __(results)__
They feel __(successful, relieved, happy about, more effective)__
My clients say: Joe is so trustworthy and smart about marketing that my sales went up 37%. [an example]

Example:
I help people create High Trust Relationships
to achieve more success and even happiness.
They feel excited and even relieved.
My clients say: "Tom coached me to get more done in 10 days than other coaches in 2 years."

Use an Empowering Question to Help Improve Your Personal Brand:
Your personal brand is your answer to the question: **"What am I best known for?"**
Your personal brand is also a promise of performance.

What can people count on you to accomplish that benefits them?

Now, here's an Empowering Question:
What do I do that's easy for me, hard for others and people want to pay for?

For the essence of Your Enchanted Prosperity, Add a Focus on Spiritual Matters

Sometimes, I talk with people who compartmentalize their brand away from their spiritual journey of life. That's not necessary—and it is *not* optimal.

When you communicate your personal brand, you are communicating how you make a contribution to other people's lives. That IS spiritual.

I was reminded of this recently. One of my Facebook friends wrote: "It's never too late to be ALIVE."

I replied, "Yes! So true. I have found that it helps to declare, *'This is the New Chapter of my life.* The previous chapter may have been full of darkness, but in this moment we walk in light and grace.'"

How can you make your personal brand a part of your daily walk in light and grace?

If you devote care and focus, you can make developing your brand an expression of part of who you really are.

Communicate the Essence of Your Brand

Author Sam Horn emphasizes what she calls an "Elevator Dialogue" (instead of the classic "Elevator Speech.") Her example is: "Have you, a family member or a friend had an MRI exam?" The person answers with details about his daughter's MRI exam. Sam's example continues with "Oh, I run the medical facilities that offer MRIs, like the one your daughter had when she hurt her knee playing soccer."

Years before I learned of Sam's example, I used dialogue on an actual elevator. I was at the university where I teach graduate students. I turned to a gentleman in the elevator.

I asked, "What do you teach?"

"Business law," he said.

"That's valuable for the students. I'm a feature film producer, I need entertainment lawyers. Have a card?"

"I'm also an agent," he continued.

"I've written and published 27 books. I'm looking to talk with agents."

He handed me two business cards. I gave him my card. This all happened before the elevator doors opened after only seconds (two floors down).

How can you communicate the essence of your brand?

_____

_____

_____

_____

_____

_____

_____

Direct Way to Increase Your Prosperity #2

No More Hesitating!—Zero-in On Your Specific Focus and Niche Business

(also known as "Jump Start the New Year!—How You Can Get Clear and Move Into Your BETTER Life")

"I'm a life coach, and I'm told that I need to focus on one niche," my client Sandra said.

"I hear you. I have three sets of questions that will help you focus on your specific area that will in turn bring you both *happiness and success.*"

"Wow! Let's do this!" Sandra said.

We'll use the G.E.T. process:

G – get clear

E – energize your difference

T – target clients you want

1. Get clear

I helped Sandra with these questions:

Niche Business Questions:

1. Who do you want to help?
2. Where's the fun?

3. In what ways is the target market similar to you?

4. How can you heal them and heal a part of you?

In our conversation, I learned that Sandra wanted to help people get beyond the dark time of intense grief.

At the end of the session, her interaction with my 4 Questions yielded: *"I want to teach women at a conference in Hawaii!"*

She was surprised at this outcome.

My job as her Executive Coach was to help her free herself from the chains of asking for too little and trying to fit into some conventional ways of thinking and being.

Now it's your turn. Imagine that you can get a big start on your path by writing out your answers (on a sheet of paper or in a journal) to these questions:

1. Who do you want to help?

2. Where's the fun?

3. In what ways is the target market similar to you?

4. How can you heal them and heal a part of you?

2. Energize your difference

Every day people are bombarded with thousands of marketing messages.

You and your work need to be different — to stand out.

I'm often asked by clients to help them come up with their niche in business — that is to make a *breakthrough* in their marketing. I introduce them to what I call **"Different, Specific, Authentic (DSA)."**

If one is going to do a workshop, it needs to be

Different – to be unique and rise above the noise in the marketplace

Specific – How will the workshop provide particular benefits?

Authentic – Are you teaching about something you

personally went through? Then you can be authentic in teaching this particular workshop. Beyond this, when I help a client develop his or her marketing campaign, we focus on what I call *"A double E"—that is, Authenticity, Evidence, Experience.* I ask questions that include:
- What do you know to be true?
- What evidence do you have that what you do works for people?
- What is your personal experience that means a lot to you? How can your hard-earned wisdom help someone else?

Now it's your turn. Take a moment. Do not start with an end result (a seminar/book/speech) first. Start with your answers to these questions:
- What do you know to be true?
- What evidence do you have that what you do works for people?
- What is your personal experience that means a lot to you? How can your hard-earned wisdom help someone else?

See how these answers serve as a launch pad.

3. Target clients you want

When working with a client, I help the person focus on what I call the *Triple-Power:*

Work you do well -> Work people will pay for -> Clients you WANT

If you do something well (for example, poetry) but no one will pay for it, you may want to do it *with* your other efforts to make a living. (It's an "AND-universe.")

Another vital element is *Clients you WANT.* Often, I hear people complain about "terrible clients."

I've learned that you can set up your business so you

work with *Clients you WANT*. I have only a few clients whom I coach. I'm so careful about the selection that I talk with their references. Why? I give a significant portion of my time, energy and life to working with a particular client. So I have a process to work only with clients I want.

One author, Rich Litvin, said, "I only coach Kings and Queens." By this, he means he only works with people who take responsibility and who do not get mired in a "blame others pattern." That approach related to "Kings and Queens" is powerful.

Now it's your turn. Use a sheet of paper. Draw and label three separate circles. "Work I do well" – "Work People will Pay For" – "Clients I WANT."

Fill in the circles with ideas.

See how some of these ideas overlap. Eventually, you can see how something can simultaneously fit all three labels.

"Anything with heart sells." – Ed Sheerin, singer/songwriter

Some might disagree with Ed Sheerin. Still, we do notice that people want to have their emotions moved. (I wrote a book entitled *Emotion-Motion Life Hacks*.)

When you feel great about what you do, you can set the potential client at ease. That's a good start!

Embrace that your life has chapters. A new chapter may begin at any time. Each chapter may involve your climb to a mountain peak. At the top of each peak, you see *new* peaks from which you can choose. Then you can travel toward the new peak you hold as your new target. Consider stepping forward. Take an action. Move beyond hesitating. Take a step.

What next small steps can you take to create more and better in your life?

Direct Way to Increase Your Prosperity #3

Ask for a Raise

"I should ask for a raise. But I'm afraid. I'm might lose my job!" my friend Jerry said.

It's a good point. If we are not skillful in how we ask for a raise, we may cause ourselves more trouble. Still, when we **strategically ask for a raise**, we feel better. We can also improve our standing in the marketplace.

We'll use the A.I.M. process

A – awaken the supervisor to your value
I – inform with evidence
M – make your "raise intention" known

1. Awaken the supervisor to your value

It's a **big error** to ask for a raise by simply telling the supervisor something like: "My kids need new shoes. I need a raise." On a certain level, the supervisor does not care about what you (or your children) need. Instead, you need to **demonstrate the value you continue to bring to the company.** The strategy is to bring your "Job Diary" and a file folder filled with evidence of your excellent performance and relevant achievements for the company.

2. Inform with evidence

Above I opened the conversation about your bringing evidence of your demonstrated performance that deserves a raise. The evidence you bring can include: a) copies of emails praising your performance and achievements, b) happy clients' emails, c) notes of times when your supervisor praised you, d) calendar details showing all the times when you worked extra hours to serve the company's vital deadlines, and e) more.

Be careful about showing the extra hours. I know a particular person "George" who got fired related to "working too many hours." How? George was supposed to accomplish certain tasks in a set amount of time (a budget for work hours). The supervisor saw the extra hours and had to retroactively give more pay to George. In the supervisor's mind, George's extra hours did NOT help. Instead it was proof that George was not as speedy as the position required (a position with hourly pay not a yearly salary).

My point is: Be careful about the evidence you show. You need to view the situation from a "supervisor's point of view." Bring evidence to show how you take initiative and how your current work does one or more of these three things that employers want:

1) you save the company money
2) you make money for the company
3) you save time for another team member so he or she makes money for the company.

3. Make your "raise intention" known

Over the years, I've asked for raises a number of times. In

short, my supervisors knew that I wanted a raise. I call that "make your raise intention known." Still, be careful! Having good timing is essential. Do *not* ask for a raise at a time when you know the company is in trouble!

In a relatively quiet time, you can ask for a raise in this manner: "I have a question. How can I earn a raise?"

You are *not* really asking (or begging) for a raise. You express your intention to EARN a raise.

What evidence can you bring to show that you are:
1) saving the company money
2) making money for the company
3) saving time for another team member so he or she makes money for the company.

_____

_____

_____

_____

_____

_____

_____

Tom Marcoux

Direct Way to Increase Your Prosperity #4

How to Expand What You Offer

"I really need to get more funds into my own business," Stephen, a member of my audience, said, at my autograph table (that's where a speaker has his or her books, DVDs, and audio programs).

"It takes a combination of listening to clients and using your imagination to project to what they can use even if your clients cannot imagine what they really need," I replied.

We'll use the W.I.N. process. When you help your clients win (in new and better ways), you will win in terms of growing your business.

W – wonder about what they need—and what they fear
I – inspire them to the next step—and next step...
N – nurture them at every turn

1. Wonder about what they need—and what they fear
If you can help someone reduce or eliminate fear, they are more likely to buy what you offer. I have seen friends buy

"insurance coverage" for their computers. Why? So they do not fear being without a computer. They are promised: "If something goes wrong with your computer, just bring it in and we'll replace it."

A number of my tech-friends suggest, "By the time, you need to replace a computer, the one you had will be so out of date so don't tie up your money in being able to swap out your current computer."

Still, we see how people are willing to pay to have their fears alleviated.

A special approach to "wonder" is to ask yourself questions including:

1. Where's the fun?
2. Where's the fun ON the journey?
3. Can I shift away from fear and toward my intuition?
4. How can I start here and now?
5. How do I invest so ultimately something becomes valuable in some way?

It may seem strange to focus on "where's the fun"—still, if there is an element of fun, you are likely to devote more energy, study and time to the new development for your business.

For example, one of my clients said, "I know I have to develop an online program so I can get more income." That might work eventually, but this particular client was much more interested in connecting with people in-person.

I replied, "You could try that. Or you might want to hold your own Meetup groups. You'll have the chance to present to more people and you'll meet a lot of qualified prospective clients."

I've noticed that some people pay contractors to build their online program, but then they procrastinate. Why? They don't want to write an online program. They want to speak! They wanted to be speakers/educators more than work as an online teacher.

I currently teach two online courses (one for graduate students). Someone asked me about teaching an online course. I replied: "All the work. None of the fun." By this I meant, I still grade papers but I do not address students in-person in a classroom (where the fun arises).

Often when you expand what you offer, it's vital to devote "massive action" to get something going. It can help to develop something *aligned* with your natural abilities—and with an element of fun.

2. Inspire them to the next step—and next step...

One of the easiest ways to increase your income is to show your client how getting more material/equipment is the next logical step. For example, one of my friends gives a speech and offers a $277 audio learning system with 12 CDs at the speaking event. Hearing her speech is the first step, and it's natural for the clients to want to deepen their use of my friend's expertise. It becomes easier for a client to want to purchase a $277 learning system instead of devoting $1,500 for a series of coaching sessions.

3. Nurture them at every turn

With a number of speakers/authors, a progression of offerings provides more and closer interactions with the author.

A progressive pattern can look like this:
Book: $15.00
Online course (special discounted offer) $29.00
Audio learning system: $277
DVD video training system: $599
Series of coaching sessions: $1500

One year of personal one-to-one coaching: $20,000

At the bottom of the above list is the most direct, in-person access to the speaker-author.

In this way, the author can "nurture the clients at every turn."

What are your first thoughts about expanding what you offer? What possible products or services might you offer?

_____

_____

_____

_____

_____

Direct Way to Increase Your Prosperity #5
(Increase Sales)

Better than Selling: "Coach to Action"

"I don't like selling. I just want to focus on coaching," my client Brenda said.

"I've got good news for you. You can transform the situation. Drop selling and we'll explore how you *'coach-to-action.'* We're going to develop ways so you can enjoy enrolling people in what you offer," I replied.

When I speak of "coach to action," I mean that you coach the person to buy your product/service (if it is a real benefit for them) or to give you a referral. We'll use the C.A.N. process:

C – concentrate and listen
A – ask
N – nurture high trust relationships

1. Concentrate and listen

Some business owners have "call reluctance"—that is, they hesitate and often fail to make necessary marketing phone calls. The solution is: You concentrate on "making the offer one you *want* to talk about."

You'll want to talk about an offer that is so compelling and attractive to your prospective client that he or she will say, "How do you do that? Tell me more."

Yes, it does take effort to craft such offers, and it takes rehearsal to communicate the offer in a clear, compelling manner.

Still, you'll feel much better when you start by looking at the situation from the prospective client's point of view.

Attract the person. How? First, make sure to ask good questions near the beginning of the interaction.

I help my clients to develop "IF – THEN patterns."

Here are examples:
- IF the prospect says, "Our last sales trainer didn't help much" THEN I ask "Oh. What didn't work for your team?"
- IF the prospect says, "I don't see how your product does anything really better than the one we already have." THEN I ask "Oh. What's not working with your current product?"

2. Ask

How do you know what is important to your prospective customer? You ask Effective Questions.

"A coach is someone who tells you what you don't want to hear, who has you see what you don't want to see, so you can be who you have always known you could be." – Tom Landry

To help your prospective customer come to a decision, you may need to coach them to see where the real problems exist. That's part of the "see what you don't want to see" situation. You can do this once you've established rapport, and the person trusts you. The truth is people often do not take action unless they "feel the pain." Still, as a coach, you're helping the person be what they have always know they could be.

3. Nurture high trust relationships

"Tell me about a good moment for you," I often say when meeting a new person and then I listen a lot.

In my book *Relax Your Way Networking*, I share my phrase: **"Impress Less, Listen More."**

The idea is that you do not have to struggle to impress the other person. Instead, strive to pay close attention and listen a lot.

"If you want other people to be happy, practice compassion. If you want to be happy, practice compassion." – The Dalai Lama

Here's one of the central ideas of *Discover Your Enchanted Prosperity:* **Money arrives through Warm Connections.** By this I mean, you develop High Trust Relationships. You look at the whole situation and not just at trying to get one sale.

Now, I'll be specific. I often follow-up a first "exploratory conversation" with an email:

Example of Tom Marcoux's Follow-up Email:

Joe,
Great to talk with you today 1/15/__ —4:42 pm.
I hear you.
I agree. No need for an ebook.
You can write an article "Top 10 Myths of ____."
You can interview top movers and shakers.
You'll have an excuse to meet with and become trusted by top people in your industry.
The material will be current and not the restating of stuff in older books. *[I'm echoing Joe's concerns.]*
Such material can be part of a guest blog article (or you

can be a guest in podcasts—this goes into your biography).

Or you can place the material in your own blog (articles can be as short as 200 words—or less. You're articulate. You could record 40 second videos.)

One of the main points we spoke of was that you need to be a "credible competitor" for the places on a panel (speaking gig) or as a featured speaker.

We need certain things in your biography.

We need a video so people can trust you and see that you're articulate.

The point is: The meeting planners have fear—because all of them have made a mistake in engaging an overbearing dimwit or a boring sleep-inducer.

That's why your biography (with credibility) and your video help you compete to get a speaking slot.

For example, here's a New 2.8 min. video that I'm using to get more people in the seats for my appearance at a Feb. Conference. http://bit.ly/1PUICUf

So I'm someone who thinks differently than you.

We didn't get to this: But what is the cost?

The real question is:

What is the cost of flailing about and losing time?

Or will you work with a strategist?—that's me.

I look forward to our next conversation.

the best to you, Joe

Tom

P.S. By the way, the above material—

think of that as part of a "proposal."   :)

[Joe had asked me to send a written proposal. I emphasized that a piece of paper is *not* what we need. I mentioned that perhaps, we need to meet in-person to find out what Joe needs so he *knows* he can trust me to help him excel and create what he *really* wants to create.]

* * * * * *

Remember the idea of "coach to action" is that the person buys or gives you referrals.

Plant the idea of giving referrals. I often say, "When I have a conversation with someone, I make sure there is a lot of value so people find it easy to give me referrals."

Coaching to action (or enrolling people in what you offer) is a process of building a High Trust Relationship.

I'm often called to help a new business owner develop a Sales Plan.

Here's an example. One client, Alphonso, wanted to get people to attend his workshops.

I demonstrated an example "staircase" of 5 Steps:

(View the "bottom stair" first which is Step 1. Then work your way upwards.)

Step 5: Phone call and close the sale.

Step 4: Email. "Gentle – Stay in Contact" – This email reminds the person that you're an expert and gives them something they can use.

Step 3: Phone call (Gentle 3rd Touch) – it's possible one may close the sale.

Step 2: The Follow-up: "A gentle 2nd Touch" via the phone or email.

Step 1: (first contact): Speak at an association meeting. Provide an "irresistible offer" so audience members sign up for an enewsletter. An irresistible offer might be access to a video series you made.

How will you transform your selling process into

"coaching to action"? Which of the ideas shared grabs your attention? What will you do now to improve your selling process?

_____

_____

_____

_____

_____

_____

One of my editors said, **"Where's the spirituality in 'coaching to action'?"**

"We *transform* our approach. We seek to serve the prospective client. If we can help him or her, then they engage our services. If we're not a match, then we can help one of their friends. A focus on service certainly has a spiritual component," I replied.

"Even better, we take the fear out of the selling process," I continued.

"How?"

"When you approach people as a coach, you avoid being overbearing like traditional salespeople. Remember you seek to offer value in the conversation. And this makes it easy for people to refer you."

Direct Way to Increase Your Prosperity #6

Ask for a Referral

"How many referrals did you ask for this week?" I asked Sharon, one of my clients.

"3, maybe 2."

"You're not sure?" I asked.

"Well, I just. Okay, I'm afraid to ask for referrals," Sharon said.

"I hear you. It can be scary. So today's session will be about how you put in a couple of systems so you easily ask for referrals," I said.

"Oh! That would help a lot," she emphasized.

We'll use the A.S.K. process:

A – awaken trust
S – seed the referral
K – kindle reciprocity

1. Awaken trust

When is it hard to ask for a referral?—when we think we're asking too soon. The solution is to awaken trust in the other person. How? You interact with the person in a trustworthy way. Also, you develop the personal brand of a trustworthy person. I've guided thousands of clients, college students and audience members in the process of T.H.O.R. for building a powerful personal brand.

T.H.O.R. stands for "Trustworthy, Helpful, Organized and Respectful." The last three items build up your reputation as a trustworthy person.

You are careful with "small things." You arrive at least a bit early for appointments. You simply do what you said you would do. You make small commitments and come through.

2. Seed the referral

"I make sure that people always get value from having a conversation with me so it's easy for them to give me referrals," I often say in a first follow-up phone call with a potential new client. I continue with, "I work by referral."

The above process is a way to "plant a seed" into the person's subconscious mind. I call that "seed the referral."

I've coached clients to set some patterns for asking for a referral. Setting the pattern helps you get over the fear or reluctance to ask.

You can use this phrase: "I'm curious—who do you know who [needs your product/service]?"

Or you might begin with "I'm wondering—who do you know who ____?"

I find that when I begin with "I'm wondering"—I am preparing myself to ask for the referral. It's like tossing a tennis ball in the air just before you hit it—as you serve the ball.

Realize that just asking for a referral will likely NOT get your the referral. Why? The person's mind often goes blank on hearing such a request. You need to help the person "open a file cabinet drawer of their memory." By this I mean, the person may know some appropriate prospect for you but the names and faces are locked away in their memory. They probably cannot readily retrieve the names. Here's an example of helping someone remember:

"Sam, I'm wondering. Who do you know who said they need to make more sales?"

"I'm not sure," Sam replies.

"You belong to an association, right?"

"Sure. The XY Association."

"Picture this. You're sitting down at a meeting. You usually sit next to the same people—yes?"

"Yeah."

"See yourself there. See their faces. Now, recall a time when one of these people said something like: 'I got to make more sales.'"

"Yes! Sarah said that about a month ago ..."

That's how you help someone remember a good candidate for a referral for you.

3. Kindle reciprocity

The Three Magic Words of Networking are: Help Them First. See if you can connect people in your own circle to each other. If you refer business to Mary, she's likely to want to return the favor. Realize that just listening to someone builds up a feeling of kinship and the opportunities to share leads to more business.

How will you rehearse asking for a referral? Write down 10 names of people who would be good candidates to give you a referral.

Direct Way to Increase Your Prosperity #7

Improve Your Marketing

"I dread marketing," Alex, one of my clients, said.

"I hear you. What does marketing mean to you?" I replied and then listened to Alex's impressions and opinions about marketing.

It was clear that Alex would do much better with a *makeover* of his thoughts and approach to marketing. We'll use the W.I.N. process. We can make marketing into truly a win-win process.

W – wake up your ideal clients
I – inspire them to raise their hand
N – nurture step by step

1. Wake up your ideal clients

A number of business owners have to pause and think (and feel their way) about what they are really selling.

When you know what you're really selling, then you can know who your ideal clients are.

I was working with my client Amanda. She was

frustrated that few people were signing up for her seminar. I said to her, "It's possible that you're talking with people who you do NOT want to be working with." She kept complaining that she was talking with unmotivated people. It became clear that her ideal clients were up and coming urban professionals who were dedicated to success and achievement. Amanda then complained, "Then I'd have to move to the top of the state."

I replied, "One of my mentors said, 'If you want fish, you have to go where the fish are.'"

Along this line, the late comedian George Carlin said, "I have to go where the audience is. They won't come over to my house."

Let's focus on these simple but essential questions: Who do you WANT to be working with? What do they absolutely need? How will your product/service give them relief from something they fear – or some pain that want to eliminate?

2. Inspire them to raise their hand

Excellent marketing entices your ideal clients to "raise their hand." By this I mean the person gets in touch with YOU because they're interested in what you're offering.

Here's an example. My client Amanda speaks at a conference and offers a menu of three free conference calls. She then gets data on which of the three topics (of the conference calls) pull in more call-listeners.

When someone attends a free conference call, they are raising their hand and demonstrating that they're interested enough to show up and hear the information you're sharing. That's valuable.

3. Nurture step by step

A number of authors talk about a "sales funnel" — that is,

you have a wide pool of potential clients. That's the top of the funnel. You bring them in and at the bottom where the funnel gets smaller, we find the good clients who sign up for what you're offering.

I'll now talk about a "marketing funnel." Again, we start with a wide top of the funnel—with lots of potential clients.

People still use direct marketing these days (sending mail strategically to a highly targeted list of red-hot prospective customers). Still, another process is to get people to come to a "squeeze page" which is a web page, only designed to capture the visitor's email address.

Usually one offers something irresistible—perhaps a series of videos designed to teach an important set of skills.

The person must give their email to get the link to start viewing the videos.

When I say "nurture step by step," I mean you start by helping the person—in effect nurturing them so they can do better in business or life. Then you guide the person with options to go deeper in training with you. The options might include an online course, or book, or audio learning system or a free first-time coaching session with you.

By the way, at the bottom of the *marketing funnel* is the highest cost, most personal option you offer—which might be private one-to-one coaching.

How will you refine your marketing? What new details will you put in place?

Direct Way to Increase Your Prosperity #8

Get Money to Work for You

"Get my money to work for me? No way! I don't have any extra cash lying around!" my friend Stephanie said.

"I hear you," I replied. Later in the conversation, Stephanie seemed to be more receptive.

I've seen clients accomplish *a lot* with *much less* money than they first thought was necessary. Additionally, a number of my former college students have raised money through crowdfunding (using websites like kickstarter.com and gofundme.com).

There are a L.O.T. more options that you might think of "at first glance." We'll use the L.O.T. process:

L – look for examples
O - open
T – target incremental steps

1. Look for examples

Some well-meaning friends will say: "It takes money to make money. Only the rich get richer."

Is that true?

If you search for examples you'll find that a number of people have found clever ways to get much done for little cash invested. For example, James Altucher devoted $500 to have five website pages designed. Then he got TheStreet.com on board. (He did hire team members from India. I have a team in India so I can relate—my other teams are in the United States of America and the United Kingdom.)

He devoted $2,000 to get the coding done.

Okay, that's $2,500. It is some money. But it was *not* the $20,000 that someone I know, "Allen," poured into Allen's website.

It may not be easy to find low cost solutions. Still, one can hire part-time contractors. It IS doable.

The point is that you "get your money to work for you" in that when you invest your money into your own business, you can make assets and create cash flow—and you can later sell your company. My point here is that we're often called to make a *"spiritual shift."* People who complain about no opportunities are stuck in a *fearful* mode of thinking. On the other hand, some people hold that Higher Power is looking out for them. There's the old phrase: "God helps those who help themselves." We might say that we're invited to keep looking for positive examples—and then to take appropriate action.

2. Open

Open your eyes to possibilities. Bypass the naysayers and find out about how real people (not naysayers' imaginings) get things done. I've advised clients and college students to get advice from people who have accomplished what you want to accomplish.

The idea of "get money to work for you" also relates to the idea of getting yourself out of the rut of only earning money by working for an hourly wage.

For example, you could write an ebook. Then, you'd hire a part-time college English instructor to edit the book. Subsequently, you could make money month after month as the ebook sells on Amazon.com. In this example, "your money worked for you" in that you did work *one time* and you used your funds to hire an editor. The ebook can now bring you money year after year.

3. Target incremental steps

Recently, I shared with a group at a networking event that I was glad that the first graphic novel, *Crystal Pegasus*, my team completed was one of simple illustrations for children.

Currently, we're working on a trilogy of graphic novels suitable for teens and adults entitled *Jack AngelSword*. The illustrators have their hands full with drawing much more complex human characters. A number of team member's worked on the face of the main character Jack. Eventually two team members were able to come up with the illustration that provides Jack's debut on page 3 of the first graphic novel.

My point is: We learn by doing. Take small steps forward and make incremental progress.

How will you take small steps forward and learn as you go? How can you get yourself out of merely earning an hourly wage? What can you do that can bring you other forms of income (ethical, legal and appropriate ways)?

Direct Way to Increase Your Prosperity #9

Use the "Power of 50"

"I just can't seem to get ahead. I don't want to have to keep working weekends and 14 hour days when I'm 67!" Miranda, an audience member, said.

In response, I shared about how one of my mentors gave me the real solution. He said, "Ideally, you need to shift from concentrating 98% of your attention on just current cash flow."

He was talking about an important point. Many entrepreneurs are so caught up with working IN their business that they are not working ON their business. When this happens you don't have a business, "you just bought yourself a job." By this I mean, you have situation in which you only trade your time for money.

The Solution is:
- Build your business so you don't always have to be there.
- Build real business assets.

Here's an example: As an Executive Coach and Spoken Word Strategist, I need to be right there with my client. In

this manner, I'm in the business of helping people transform their lives! Still, every week, I schedule time for:
- I'm writing—toward my next books (I don't have to be there as the books sell in 15 countries)
- Work on my franchise *Jack AngelSword*.

For example, my 29th book *Droids to Magic: Fantastic Tales of Science Fiction and Wonder* debuted on Amazon.com.

Droids to Magic features characters from two of my franchises: *Jack AngelSword* and *Jenalee Storm*. These franchises will ultimately include graphic novels, feature films and action figures!

The Power of Exceptional Focus:

Do you spend time each week, actually building your business? Or are you—what I called myself years ago—"a little fire truck putting out fires?"

Improve your life. How? Use what I call the *Power of 50*. The ideal ratio of working on current cash flow and working on building your business is 50%-50%. Or what I call the Power of 50.

It's true that your percentages of working on current cash flow and working on future cash flow will vary week to week.

Still, it helps to keep that idea of 50%-50% in mind. With my company, I devote time to building assets—in our case these are intellectual properties or "franchises." Ultimately, I want my franchises (*Jack AngelSword, Jenalee Storm, TimePulse, Crystal Pegasus*) to serve so many people that Disney wants to buy my company near the end of my lifespan. I want my work to continue to inspire and entertain people beyond my lifespan.

How can you devote more time to creating assets?

Protect and Build Your Energy #1

Find Out How You're Two Simple Steps Away from More Success and Happiness

"I'm afraid that my business will go under," Andrea, an audience member, told me after I gave a speech.

"I can help you with that. First, we can use your fear as a warning system. It's the indicator button so we can do something different from this moment forward," I replied.

As an Executive Coach and Spoken Word Strategist, I use a particular skill: asking Empowering Questions.

Here are three helpful ones:
- Are you hiding?
- What do you need to let go?
- Is it time to adapt or accept?

1. Are you hiding?

Many business owners hide and do something, anything, other than what's necessary to sell their products or services.

This is the reason that I emphasize the practice of "See the Three" (this is one of my *Emotion-Motion Life Hacks*—from my book of the same name.)

The idea is to **See the Three Simple Measurements.**

This week how many
- referrals did you ask for?
- times did you ask for a sale?
- "sales conversations" did you have?

Now it's your turn.
What can be your Three Simple Measurements?
You can apply the measurements to your business and even to your personal life. Are you having a date night twice a month with your romantic partner?

What do you need to let go?

Are you holding on to old pain?

An important question is: *What are you filling this present moment with?*

Some days ago, an elderly relative said some really mean things—over the phone.

The next morning I woke up with this phrase in my thoughts: "End it. Get up easy."

Now, I'm not going to end my relationship with that bitter, elderly relative. But I'm going to *end my ruminating* about that person today!

And then I "get up easy." I raise the level of my thoughts. I think of being kind to everyone I'm in contact with today. I fill my present moment with hope, kindness and positive action.

Here's the truth: *If you do not let go, you're likely to leak energy.* Then you may not have the energy to face what you've been hiding from.

So the questions "What do you need to let go?" and "Are you hiding?" connect to help you take your life to higher levels of success and happiness.

Now it's your turn.

What do you need to let go?

Do you need to understand that some people will NOT change? They have no interest in changing.

Do you need to become more skillful in shifting your thoughts so you raise the level of your current mood?

2. Is it time to adapt or accept?

"What can I do when things feel out of my control?" Amy, a client, asked me.

When we feel that we have no control in a situation, we can Adapt or Accept.

Acceptance does NOT mean approval. It means that you just stop resisting. Resisting uses up a lot of energy.

After we stop resisting, we can decide about our *response*. I use three words to remind me of a good action to take "kind, healthy, holy."

A number of people have told me that they prefer substituting "spiritual" for the word "holy." I use the word "holy" because it's easy to remember.

Recently, I posted a comment in social media. I wrote:

"During this season, I wish you loving, happy moments. One of the best ideas I've heard is *"To love is to be happy with."* – *Barry Neal Kaufman* ... Let's devote some moments to truly listen to friends and family. I like to say, "Tell me about a good moment for you." Then I listen a lot.

many blessings"

I was surprised when I saw this response:

"This is without a doubt, the most decent and civilized post I have seen, maybe ever. – Marty D. (posted 12/24/15 – 7:44 AM on Google+

* * *

This section is about "Find Out How You're 2 Simple Steps Away from More Success and Happiness."

Here are the Steps:

Step #1: Ask an Empowering Question.

Step #2: Take a small action in the positive direction that your answer(s) illuminate.

What Empowering Question would help you at this time? How can you take small actions to get yourself moving in a positive direction?

_____

_____

_____

_____

Protect and Build Your Energy #2

What Will Change Your Life Forever?

"I'm really suffering now," my close friend, Sharon, said.

I listened to her for an extended time.

Often, having someone simply listen closely will help a person.

This time Sharon asked me, "You're the expert on this. What can help me change my situation? What would you advise?"

I looked her in the eyes and said with compassion: "Part of what I do is connect with my intuition and ask the useful questions in the moment. It's not about my providing an answer. It's about my setting the stage for the client to find her own answers."

Here's a valuable question.

What will change your life forever? Two things:
- YOUR answer to an Empowering Question
- YOUR Want-Power ignited

1) YOUR answer to an Empowering Question
As an Executive Coach, I'm working with clients every

week and helping them take consistent and wise action.

How do you get access to your inner wisdom? Connect with Empowering Questions.

You can combine questions and answers.

For example, my client Miranda answered the following questions in this way:
- What's the most important thing for you to be doing right now? [Get more clients.]
- Are you hiding from something? [My allowing everything else to take me away from devoting one hour per day to make marketing phone calls.]
- Are you letting fear run your life? [Yes. I'm afraid of being rejected on the phone. I'm afraid of bothering people. I'm afraid of hurting my reputation.]
- What small action can you take now to act with courage? [I can write a list of 10 people to call. I can write down how I can be gracious on the phone. I can write down how I can make offers that are filled with benefits that potential clients WANT. I can rehearse phone calls with my coach.]

Now, it's your turn.

Write down your own answers to these Empowering Questions:
- What's the most important thing for you to be doing right now?
- Are you hiding from something?
- Are you letting fear run your life?
- What small action can you take now to act with courage?

2) YOUR Want-Power ignited

Many of us have fallen into a notion that we just "need to increase personal willpower."

I've learned that there's something much more powerful than willpower: It's WANT-Power.

By this I mean, **you make big efforts and endure fear and setbacks if you really want something!**

For example, I wanted to walk on the bottom of the ocean. But then I got in a ride called *Mission: Space* at Walt Disney World. You get in a "can" that they spin so the centrifugal force simulates taking off in a rocket. In that can, I felt shaken to my core by claustrophobia. How would I endure putting on a helmet (to walk on the ocean floor) that would get me feeling claustrophobic?

Did I let that stop me from donning a helmet and walking on the bottom of the ocean? No! I *rehearsed* walking with a helmet on by wearing a sweatshirt with a hood. I imagined and visualized walking on the ocean bottom. I learned that **the answer to fear is rehearsal.**

Then I went out and put a helmet on and walked on the bottom of the ocean. How? Because I *wanted* to walk on the ocean floor since I was 8 years old and saw the film *20,000 Leagues Under the Sea*.

Can you imagine the strength of WANT-Power?

Whoever is devoid of the capacity to wonder, whoever remains unmoved, whoever cannot contemplate or know the deep shudder of the soul in enchantment, might just as well be dead for he has already closed his eyes upon life. - Albert Einstein

Let's focus on *"know the deep shudder of the soul in enchantment."* When I speak on *Discover Your Enchanted Prosperity*, I emphasize that we CAN find what makes our heart sing. Many of us can bring more prosperity into our lives when we connect with what means much to our deepest heart. And *this is the essence of Want-Power.*

Singer/composer Tori Amos and saxophonist Kenny G both had success with their *second* music album only after they made music arising from *their inner guidance* (or personal intuition).

In his TEDx Talk, Adam Leipzig gave an example of telling someone what you do—connected to one's life purpose: "I help people get their greatest work into the world."

I share this example because clearly expressing what you do that aligns with your heart (and that is some form of contribution to humankind) brings real power.

Here's another example: If someone asks me about my work as an Executive Coach and Spoken Word Strategist, I say, "I help people create High Trust Relationships to gain more success and the Golden Yes!"

Now, the question is: "How do you ignite WANT-Power?"

I'll demonstrate this as *a process of answering specific questions for yourself.*

As I mention in other sections of this book, for someone who wants to create his or her own business, I provide these questions:

1. Who do you want to help?
2. Where's the fun?
3. In what ways is your target market similar to you?
4. How can you heal them and a part of you?

Which Empowering Questions will you use as springboards to changing your life? How will you use WANT-power to give you the energy and persistence to move forward?

Protect and Build Your Energy #3

Fill Your Mind with What Empowers You

Two of my favorite quotes are:
- *Replace worry with action. – Steve Chandler*
- *Money does not corrupt; mindset corrupts. You can have money AND have a generous, abundant, uncorrupted mindset. – Julie Ann Cairns*

A mindset of worry does much to corrupt a person. It robs you of energy. It restricts your viewpoint and options. It sets you on edge and engenders irritation and frustration.

The real solution is to fill your mind with SOMETHING OTHER than worry.

1. Replace worry with action.
I talk about this elsewhere in this book. Here I want to emphasize that I personally know the power of repeating "Replace worry with action" in my own mind. Since I'm working with teams and various projects, it is a temptation to fall into a spiral of worry. Instead, I lead myself and my

team members to the next positive action. When you take an action, however small, you'll find that you simply feel better . . . and you create *real progress*.

2. Build Your Empowered Mindset
An Empowered Mindset can be built on:
- focus on creativity
- devotion to service
- quieting down fear
- a prayer "for my good and the good of all involved"

Use this question to help you make better choices: **"Does this strengthen me?"**

Using that question can help you:
- drop destructive habits
- reduce time with negative people (even some relatives)
- drop watching disempowering TV shows

Let's return to the quote "Money does not corrupt; mindset corrupts."

When you take action with more care to empower your mindset, you can nourish your mindset with
- positive audio programs and books
- laughter
- exercise
- quiet time (prayer, meditation and other activities)
- fun!

How will you take great care of yourself? How will you empower your mindset?

Protect and Build Your Energy #4

Live Fearlessly

"I feel stuck," my friend Kathy said. "I can help with that," I replied. During our discussion, I asked, "So how are you with fear in your life?"

Stuck and fear are related.

As an Executive Coach and Spoken Word Strategist, I help clients frequently rise above fear. We'll use the C.A.N. process:

C – change the frame
A – assess your "Fearless-Action"
N – nurture yourself

1. Change the frame

How does fear paralyze us? It controls how we "frame a situation" — in other words, how we *perceive* a situation.

If we see a situation with "the eyes of fear" our vision is *restricted*.

Worse than that, we cannot see ourselves adapting and succeeding during a crucial event or moment.

I've seen people fail to return a phone call or even send a resume due to personal fear.

It helps to consciously reframe one's thoughts and point of view.

For example, when I first aimed to get speaking engagements (some years ago), I was afraid of not having the "perfect" video, articles and supporting material in my speaker's kit.

Then I learned to transform my view of the situation from "they rejected me" or "they will reject me" to a *new frame* of "We did not have a match" and "It is all good practice."

This process is also known as "reframing."

How do you live fearlessly? You "fear" less.

By this I mean: "Turn down the volume on fear."

I'm often traveling in a car with a team member on my way to give a speech.

My team member likes to have music playing on the radio.

Often, I have moments in which I turn down the radio volume.

This is a good metaphor. In life, **I turn down the fear and turn UP the rehearsal.**

So in the car, I turn down the radio volume and rehearse for my upcoming speech.

Instead of ruminating over my fear of making any error in speaking, I fill up my thoughts and consciousness with excellent rehearsal.

I give fear LESS space in my conscious mind.

Now it's your turn.

How can you turn down the volume of your personal fear? How can you rehearse or prepare—and focus on that process of making yourself ready and capable of excellent performance?

2. Assess your "Fearless-Action"

Ask yourself: "What would I do if I was not stopped by fear?"

Early in my business career, I found myself failing to ask for referrals.

Then I learned to query myself with: **"What would I do if I was not stopped by fear?"**

The answer was: "I'd ask for a referral."

So I discovered something useful: I could **assess what would be my "Fearless-Action."** This is the action I would take if fear were absent.

[This became part of my program "Get Clients Fearlessly."]

Now it's your turn.

What would you do—perhaps, a small action—if fear was not present nor was it holding you back? How can you take a small action in the fearless direction?

3. Nurture yourself

To act in a fearless (or *"not encumbered by fear"*) manner, you need lots of personal energy. To stretch in your life, takes energy and strength.

Imagine how many times we fail to take the courageous action because "I'm so tired" or "I don't feel strong enough." We may feel that we're too tired to be able to "think on our feet."

Much of the process for creating more success in our lives requires quick adapting and thinking on one's feet.

I speak often in front of groups—so I rehearse often.

In fact, before every networking event I practice my answer to this question: "Tom, what do you do?"

My answer is: "I help people create High Trust Relationships so they gain more success and the Golden Yes."

I remember the first time I asked for a fee of $400 per hour. To deal with any fear, I rehearsed saying that amount firmly and smoothly. Was I scared? Sure. Was I well-rehearsed? YES.

More than that, I made sure to take a walk and relax before I placed the important phone call.

Be sure to nurture yourself.

I remember attending a special event and listening to author Zig Ziglar saying: "If you had a thoroughbred racehorse, would you feed him junk food and deny him sleep? Of course not. You would take good care of him!"

Yes—let's treat ourselves at least as well as a horse!

Now it's your turn.

How can you nurture yourself and build up a reserve of personal energy?

* * *

To live fearlessly means that you consciously work to "fear" less.

Quiet down fear. Turn the fear volume down.

Do not wait for the absence of fear.

Instead, fill your mind with empowering thoughts, plans and action.

We can use fear as a signal for more preparation and rehearsal.

That's useful.

Beyond that, fill your life with action and aiming for what you truly want.

"Courage is not the absence of fear but rather the judgment that something is more important than fear." – Meg Cabot

You can enjoy more moments of the day focused on progress and moving forward.

How can you build up your personal energy? Then you'll be more likely to avoid giving into fear.

_____

_____

_____

_____

_____

_____

_____

_____

Protect and Build Your Energy #5

How You Can Cope When the Worst Happens

It all hit at once: I was sick and rundown; my father fell ill, landing in the hospital—and miles away—my frail, elderly mother needed care. Oh—and just before that, I had to give a speech when my voice was failing.

I share this to give you the context that I'm speaking from experience about *coping during high pressure times.*

Many of us seek to make our dreams come true. To make continual progress and avoid being derailed, it's vital for us to become skilled at enduring the toughest moments of life.

We'll discuss the O.W.N. process.

O – open

W – warm up support/relationships

N – nurture yourself

I use the word "OWN" related to how we do better to keep up our OWN self-care practices.

1. Open

You can use your mind to help you during your difficult

time. How? Train yourself to shift to better thoughts and feeling that can empower you. The process is to pick a phrase (what I call a "SwitchPhrase") to shift the direction of your thoughts. This phrase can be used to switch the direction of your "train of thoughts."

It's easy to start having catastrophic thoughts. To counteract that tendency, I use this phrase: "I'll enter the moment fresh."

For example, I have endured situations in which I need to deal with a particular bitter, elderly relative. Instead of losing my energy ahead of time to worrying about how painful the upcoming interaction might be, I tell myself "I'll enter the moment fresh."

The idea here is open yourself to good possibilities instead of closing down on negative preconceptions.

I admit that over the years some thoughts arose like "Nothing I do will be good enough for that bitter, elderly relative." But then I catch myself and say, "I'll enter the moment fresh." I further encourage myself by thinking: "I'll do what I can. That will be good. I'll give myself acknowledgement and approval for my own good efforts."

Another way that "open" is an empowering approach during a tough time relates to quiet time, gratitude and prayer.

"If the only prayer you ever say in your entire life is thank you, it will be enough." – Meister Eckhart

Devoting even just a moment can shift your perspective. During the toughest moments of my life, I've had the love and support of my sweetheart and friends. That's a lot to be grateful for. Researchers have noted that it takes 10 seconds of attention so that a positive detail becomes part of our long term memory. So I write in my *Daily Journal of Victories and Blessings* every night just before sleep—to devote time for paying attention and feeling grateful.

Gratitude unlocks the fullness of life. It turns what we have into enough, and more. – Melody Beattie

It takes personal discipline to turn one's attention to gratitude—when we're enduring a tough time. Still, we can choose to expand our awareness with gratitude. And, with gratitude we can brighten our perspective.

"Better keep yourself clean and bright; you are the window through which you must see the world." – George Bernard Shaw

2. Warm up support/relationships

If possible, when things are quieter (not a worst time), do what you can to support your current relationships. Be kind. Express appreciation. Help people close to you. Build up your emotional bank accounts (that's a metaphor for how you can be kind and "make a deposit" into a relationship).

During your difficult time, take care of yourself. I keep a log of my sleep. Sleep will help you have more patience, and that can help you have the energy to express appreciation to anyone who helps you: friends, nurses, doctors, family members and others. When you are kind, it's amazing how people near you (for the most part) will reflect your sunny attitude back to you.

2. Nurture yourself

Taking good care of yourself is critical for you to navigate a difficult time with grace. Do what you can to get help so you can get sleep when possible. Additionally, make efforts to keep "something normal" in your day. My normal day includes quiet time with assembling a jigsaw puzzle and music. So during tough times, I enjoy even just 9 minutes of that activity so my subconscious mind does not feel that the whole world is upside down.

I also make sure to get in a 15 minute walk—at least.

Be sure to schedule breaks for yourself. I alert my friends that I may want to call them and talk about anything other than my parents' health issues—to give me some time away from the continuing difficulties.

Make sure to devote time with a beloved cat or dog—or other furry friend.

I work with my own coach. You may find it valuable to work with a counselor or therapist. Often a loved one who is having a physical crisis withdraws emotionally from us. So we need emotional support. Be sure to have someone who can really listen to you. Sometimes, it's crucial to hire real support from a mental health professional.

* * *

My intention has been to provide a brief section that brings up a few critical self-care practices for when you're enduring the worst.

You might find it valuable to read books or listen to audiobooks on the topics of self-care during difficult times.

You need to be strong. You need to OWN your self-care practices and keep them going. You need them now more than ever before.

Time devoted to self-care is vital.

I recall the military idea: "More sweat in training. Less blood in battle."

We might adapt this as **"More healthy self-care; More**

grace during difficult times."
Many blessings to you.

How can you nurture yourself so you have more energy to devote to your efforts to increase your prosperity?

_____

_____

_____

_____

_____

_____

_____

_____

Protect and Build Your Energy #6

How to Take Inspired Action (Manifest What You Want in the New Year)

"I want so much, but I'm afraid," my client Miranda said.
"Afraid of what?" I asked.
"Afraid that this year won't be different than last year. That it will be more of the same pain," she said.
We talked some more then I said, "This reminds me of a recent visit I had at a friend's house. While I was in the restroom, they set up dinner. I arrived at the table and the mother, father and daughter were eating pizza.
I had a bite of the pizza. The take-out pizza was burnt. I stopped eating.
I saw the father scrape off some cardboard from the pizza box on his slice of pizza. He told himself, "It's okay."
I do have hope for this family because, with my support, the daughter called the pizza restaurant and reported the burnt pizza.
"All she had to do was ASK. Her family had paid for the pizza. The pizza restaurant employee immediately said,

'We'll make you two new pizzas.' So she got in the car and got the replacement pizzas. What do you get from my story, Miranda?"

"All you have to do is ask," Miranda replied.

"Yes. And **you don't have to eat burnt pizza**. Do you see how this has bearing on how you will make this New Year a better year than before?"

To make your New Year better, learn to **take Inspired Action.** We'll use the A.I.M. process:

A – assess "Love or Fear"
I – inquire
M – make your heart-response loud

1. Assess "Love or Fear"

For some of us the idea "love or fear" seems vague or strange.

We can try these questions:
- Am I doing this because I'm afraid something will happen? (fear)
- Am I doing this because I hope something will happen and I think it will help someone? (love)

When I talk about "Inspired Action," I'm referring to taking action that arises from inspiration from your own Higher Self—and for those of us who focus on the spiritual—from inspiration from Higher Power.

In over 14 years of teaching college level Comparative Religion (from an online course that I wrote), I've observed that **many spiritual paths emphasize "approach life with love."**

By the way, to get the replacement pizza (for the burnt pizzas), the daughter talked with love: That is, she simply mentioned the burnt pizza in a calm tone. She made a space for the pizza restaurant employees to improve the situation.

Now it's your turn.

Can you direct your efforts in ways to help others? Can you be kind to yourself (that's a loving approach)? Where is the "burnt pizza" in your life? What can you do to drop "burnt pizza" from your life and make room for new blessings? Is your approach one of kindness and compassion?

2. Inquire

It's true that at various times, we don't know what's the best thing to do next.

Focus on this idea: Inquire. Ask questions.

Stephen, one of my clients, said, "I know I should set up an online course but I don't know which topic I should choose. I could work hard and hire a tech person—and no one may sign up for a course I wrote. I'd just lose money."

"I hear you," I said. "It helps to 'inquire.' You can ask people through social media: 'Which of these 3 topics would you sign up for a free conference call?' From the responses you might be guided to create an online course on one of the three topics. Or none of them. Then you try something else."

I invited Stephen to notice his own responses to the feedback he received. If he got excited that people were responding to a particular topic, this might demonstrate that *his Inspired Action* would be to pursue making an online course on that particular topic.

Now it's your turn.

Are you inquiring/asking questions in your daily life? Or

are you "flying blind?" If you serve customers, it helps to find out what they prefer. How do you know? Ask.

For taking Inspired Action, ask yourself: How can I transform what I do to focus in the following Three Areas?

- the kind thing to do
- the healthy thing to do
- the holy thing (spiritual/kind/compassionate/what Higher Power would ask for) to do.

3. Make your heart-response loud

I remember a line of dialogue from a *STAR TREK* feature film.

Captain Kirk wanted to use a starship to travel to two planets in efforts to restore his friend Spock to life. He asked the officials if he could do that.

He returned from the meeting, and Lieutenant Sulu asked: "The word, sir? "

Captain Kirk replied, "The word ... is no. **I am therefore going anyway."**

The movie theater audience cheered. I admit it: I cheered, too.

To take Inspired Action is NOT about waiting for approval or agreement. What counts MORE is your "heart-response."

The idea here is your heart-response is more important than any advice you might be given.

As an Executive Coach, I speak on *Discover Your Enchanted Prosperity* because I do more than help people solve problems. I help them transform their lives. This involves getting access to intuition and one's heart-response.

Now it's your turn.

What does YOUR heart want? How can you quiet down the distractions in your life so you can hear your own heart-response?

Who is telling you "no"? How can you go around them? How can you take an appropriate risk? How can you take Inspired Action?

When you act with the approach of love, you calmly, pleasantly ask for what you want. To improve this year, make warm connections. In a friendly tone, ask for referrals or sales (if you run a business).

With friends and family, in a compassionate tone, ask to develop agreements. This is better than building up resentments by holding only expectations about other people.

This New Year is full of positive potential.
The universe asks that you take Inspired Action.

What do you imagine might be Inspired Action for you to take? How might you do something new and bring new and better into your life?

_____

_____

_____

_____

_____

_____

Protect and Build Your Energy #7

How You Can Use Hidden Power— Be an *OptiRealist Leader*

"The people at work are stuck," my client Tina said.

"How much do you want things to improve?" I asked.

"A lot. I'm so drained when I get home," she replied.

"There are things you can do to subtly shift the energy. That's when you become an *OptiRealist Leader*," I said.

The term *OptiRealist Leader* is one of my favorites that I have coined.

As you can guess, I have combined "optimist" and "realist" to form the word "OptiRealist."

Optimism is valuable. For example, Steve Jobs was optimistic that his team could ensure that people could get to their music in "just three clicks." Jobs had to *convince* his team that this was possible with the first iPod.

Similarly, without optimism and a vision, people do NOT put forth effort. Still, optimism is *not* enough. "Blind optimism" led to the deaths of eight people during a Mt. Everest climb. They faced a choice. Take a risk and climb toward the summit late in the day or wait to the next day.

Unfortunately, according to a number of authors, this team chose poorly. It would have been wise to postpone the climb. Instead, after they summited Mt. Everest, they climbed down in the dark, and eight people lost their lives.

So the real empowering leader is one who uses the tenets of *OptiRealist Leadership*.

We'll use the A.I.M. process:

A – aspire

I – intensify nurturing

M – measure

1. Aspire

To *aspire* means "to seek to attain or accomplish a particular goal." (merriam-webster.com)

One of my favorite examples of a leader inspiring his group to aspire is when Mark Burnett, creator of the TV Show *Survivor* faced the problem of having no where to house his crew and equipment in a remote tropical location. His crew said, "We'll have to pick somewhere else to shoot this season's episodes." Burnett said, "We are going to solve this. Give me some ideas." Eventually one team member suggested that they hire a cruise ship—which is like a floating city. All provisions were on the cruise ship, and the crew used a speed boat to travel between ship and shore.

The OptiRealist Leader provides the direction.

It helps to communicate clearly *and* provide space for people to offer supportive ideas.

The OptiRealist Leader begins with: "I'll now share three ideas about how we can solve the XY problem." (We refer to this as a "headline.")

Then the OptiRealist Leader says, "After I share the three ideas, I'm going to open this up. I want to hear your ideas, thoughts and feelings about this. *Together* we'll come up with something excellent."

Now it's your turn. How can you communicate clearly and keep the space for people to share ideas?

2. Intensify nurturing

A great leader is an excellent listener who nurtures and empowers the team member. Such listening enhances the leader/team member relationship.

Nurture talent.

I learned two things from directing feature films: a) Protect the Talent and b) Guard Momentum.

In filmmaking, the talent is the group of actors (male and female).

The cinematography and screenplay mean nothing if the actors fail to give credible, moving performances.

So the OptiRealist Leader makes sure that team members have what they need to perform well.

Additionally, the OptiRealist Leader nurtures or guards the momentum of the project. A major project is like a train. It takes significant effort to get the project rolling. The OptiRealist Leader makes sure to keep the team flowing forward well.

Now it's your turn. Are you expressing appreciation for team members' contributions?

3. Measure

An old phrase is: "You can't improve it if you can't measure it."

The OptiRealist Leader zeroes in on the most meaningful measurements.

With my clients who own businesses, I help them "See the

Three."

For a business owner, the Three Measurements are embodied in these questions:

This week –

a. how many referrals did I ask for?

b. how many sales conversations did I have?

c. how many times did I ask someone to buy something?

The OptiRealist Leader also watches measurements in order to avoid "holding the 'Wrong B.A.G.'"

I coined this phrase B.A.G. as in *Blind Adherence to Goal*.

At the beginning of this section, I mentioned the eight Mt. Everest climbers who lost their lives. According to a number of authors, they made a poor decision. They kept to a deadly goal. We can call this "Blind Adherence to Goal."

Sometimes, the marketplace may show us that our goal or approach is faulty. **The OptiRealist Leader pays close attention.**

As an Executive Coach, my job is to keep my eyes wide open and *help clients open their eyes, too.*

As we get feedback from the marketplace, we adjust and improve the project. Or we even throw out the wrong project. We avoid "Blind Adherence to a Goal."

How do you know?

The OptiRealist Leader "knows the numbers." He or she knows how many marketing calls leads to one in-person appointment—for example.

Also the OptiRealist Leader is ready to throw out "the old way of doing things" when conditions have changed.

Combining optimism and realism gives the OptiRealist Leader an edge.

As an Executive Coach, I speak on *Discover Your Enchanted Prosperity*. If you seek to create a company or improve the performance of your current company, it helps to remember A.I.M.: Aspire; Intensify Nurturing; and Measure.

To make a breakthrough, here are helpful questions: Are you doing what is necessary? What will you change? Are you focusing on your purpose?

_____

_____

_____

_____

_____

_____

_____

_____

_____

Protect and Build Your Energy #8

Get Real or Get Hurt—Get the False Stuff Out of Your Way—and Then Succeed

"Tell me something you know to be true, Tom," my long-time friend Sara asked.

"You need a good combination of optimism AND realism to do well in life. That's why I refer to myself as an OptiRealist," I replied.

I decided to write a speech on this topic:
"Get Real or Get Hurt:
How You Can Get False Stuff Out of Your Way
and
Create the Abundance, Success and Happiness You Want"

Reading many books each year, I'm drawn to those authors who tell the unvarnished truth. Why? So I can Save Time, Save Efforts, Save Money and . . . protect myself in certain situations.

That's why the topic "Get Real or Get Hurt" arose in my thoughts.

About "False Stuff," we can lose time, money and tears when we get caught up in false ideas, false methods and even false friends.

"It ain't what you don't know that gets you into trouble. It's what you know for sure that just ain't so." – ascribed to Mark Twain

I know the power of optimism. Without optimism, we do not put in efforts.

For example, I know someone, Eric, who had the optimism and vision that earning a masters degree in illustration would help him in his career. It's working. Eric is one of my team members working on my graphic novels entitled *Jack AngelSword*.

Still, we need strategies and realism to endure and triumph over the setbacks in life.

A novice speaker asked me if one needed academic degrees to be a professional speaker. I replied that a speaker needs Authenticity, Evidence and Experience. (I noted this as "A double E" — referring to A.E.E.)

My work is built on experience *not* theory.

In this section, I'll share a portion of my "Get Real or Get Hurt" speech.

The structure I use is:
- Myth
- A Way You Can Get Hurt
- The Get Real Principle

Myth #1: If you do the right things, you can rest in the idea that your friends will stay for a lifetime.

A Way You Can Get Hurt:

You'll waste time and you'll lose personal energy in trying to please people who really cannot support you and cannot understand you.

The Get Real Principle:
Be different—be YOU.

I learned the hard way that doing my best and doing a lot of listening to some individuals is *not* valued by them. One friend (who drifted away) told me at the end of a phone conversation: "That was largely useless."

I replied, "I do *not* do useless things. I care about you. If you have an emergency, feel comfortable to call me. But I will not be calling you."

This decision to separate from this friend did not arrive lightly to me. I had made efforts over more than two decades to keep being a good friend and keep listening. The truth was: this person did not value my listening. It was time to let the person drift away.

So I came up with this paragraph:

Some friendships are novels.
Some friendships are short stories.
Some friendships are a sentence.
Put a period on that and get away!

The Get Real Principle is "Be different—be YOU."
When you are genuine and you support your real self then you simply feel better.

You avoid twisting yourself for other people's approval. You'll have real friendships. You'll be strong, and you'll be okay if some friendships turn out to be short stories. When you step into a new chapter of life, not all of your friends will want to go with you.

Still, if you treat yourself like a cherished friend, you'll enjoy more moments of happiness and even success.

Now it's your turn.

Do you have any friendships that are truly unhealthy for you? What truth do you need to face? Do you need to limit your exposure to some negative people (even certain relatives)?

* * * * * *

Myth #2: You can make good money at just about anything.

A Way You Can Get Hurt:
You can lose a lot of time doing projects that do not yield excellent results because the pattern is self-defeating.

The Get Real Principle:
Have a Good Business Model.

A close friend (I'll call him "George") died under tough circumstances. In his 60s, George struggled to barely pay his rent each month. Why? His business model was garbage. By this I mean, he was working too hard for too little return. There was no way to get ahead.

George wrote press releases. I'd ask him, "Can you go back to your previous clients and see if they have more work for you?"

"No," George replied. He explained that he could write the best press release, but if something startling happened in the news, his press release could be ignored. George was leaving a trail of unhappy clients.

"George, you've been a journalist for so long." I began.

"You know how to coach someone to do well with the press, TV interviews and more. How about building up that end of your business?"

Sadly, George just "didn't get around to" making the needed changes in his Business Model (his system for earning income and running his business).

George struggled greatly until his last breath on earth.

I helped George—for example, transporting him to the hospital and staying with him for five hours. Still, his business model was doing him in.

On the other hand, a good business model looks like this:
- *You can get repeat business.*
- *You're expanding how you serve clients.*
- *You're building assets.*

For example, my team works on my franchises (the assets): *Jack AngelSword, Jenalee Storm, TimePulse* and *Crystal Pegasus*. If you're curious, see the *Crystal Pegasus* graphic novel on Amazon.com. Franchises are often built on intellectual property.

(A mnemonic device is "REB"—related to Repeat Business, Expand, Build Assets.)

Here's an example of "REB." I had the idea for a particular speech title. In the same week, I set an engagement to speak on that topic at a conference. Then in 30 days, I had a book completed and up on Amazon.com—on that new topic.

* * * * * *

Above, I've shared a part of my speech "Get Real or Get Hurt." (In a sense, this speech continues the work of my book *Darkest Secrets of Persuasion and Seduction Masters: How to Protect Yourself and Turn the Power to Good*.) In this section and at my blog YourBodySoulandProsperity.com, I write about practical ways one can increase prosperity. It does not have to be a serious, dreadful journey. **I hold to the idea of having a light heart and enjoying some laughter each day.**

Still, it's valuable to face reality and strategically act for your benefit and others.

Yes, I am an OptiRealist.

As an Executive Coach, I do a lot to help my clients use the strength of optimism and the effectiveness of realism to make their dreams come true. I often function as coach, consultant and mentor. I save my clients lots of time, effort and tears. My clients then get to focus their personal energy to leap forward faster. One client said, "Tom Marcoux coached me to get more done in 10 days than other coaches in 2 years!" – Brad Carlson, CEO of MindStrong, LLC.

Find your way to balance optimism and realism for your journey.

How will you build assets — and get repeat business?

_____

_____

_____

_____

_____

A FINAL WORD AND SPRINGBOARD TO YOUR DREAMS

Congratulations on your efforts as your worked with the material in this book. To get even more value from this book, take the plans and insights that you created and place them in some form in your calendar or day planner. *Plan and take action.* Return to these pages again and again to reconnect with the material and take your life to higher levels.

The best to you,
Tom

Tom Marcoux
Executive Coach - Spoken Word Strategist

Special Offer Just for Readers of this Book:

Contact Tom Marcoux at tomsupercoach@gmail.com for special discounts on **coaching**, books, workshops and presentations. Just mention your experience with this book.

==> See an Excerpt from Tom Marcoux's book, *Darkest Secrets of Persuasion and Seduction Masters: How to Protect Yourself and Turn the Power to Good* – on the next page.

Excerpt from
Darkest Secrets of Persuasion and Seduction Masters: How to Protect Yourself and Turn the Power to Good
by Tom Marcoux, Executive Coach – Spoken Word Strategist
Copyright Tom Marcoux

... Now, I am in my 40's, with gray in my hair, and for 27 years I have been taking action to protect people.

And now is the time for me to protect you with the Countermeasures I reveal in this book.

Every human being needs to be able to break the trance that a Manipulator creates.

You need to make good decisions so you are safe and you keep growing — and you are not cut down and crippled.

This Darkest Secrets material is so intense that I first released it only with the counterbalance of my most energizing and uplifting books, *Nothing Can Stop You This Year!* and *10 Seconds to Wealth: Master the Moment Using Your*

Divine Gifts.

An interviewer asked me: "Who can be the Manipulator?"

A co-worker, a boss, a salesperson, someone you're dating, and someone you think is a friend.

Now is the time—this very minute—for me to write this book to protect you.

I must speak the truth.

These Darkest Secrets of "persuasion masters" are ...

Wait a minute! Let's say it plainly: These are the Darkest Secrets of masters of manipulation. Throughout this book, I will call these people what they are: Manipulators.

Dictionary.com defines "manipulate" as "To influence or manage shrewdly or deviously.... To tamper with or falsify for personal gain."

In this book, we will look on a manipulator as one who deviously influences someone with no concern about that person's well-being, and who causes harm to that person.

Here is the first Darkest Secret:

Darkest Secret #1:
Manipulators Make You Hurt
and Then Offer the Salve.

Manipulators would invite you to go out in the sun for hours and then sell you the salve to soothe your burns. The problem is that we don't notice that this is what they're doing.

For example, you're considering the purchase of a house. A Manipulator asks the question, "So, where would you put your TV?" This question is designed to put you into a trance.

Dictionary.com defines "trance" as "a half-conscious state, seemingly between sleeping and waking, in which ability to function voluntarily may be suspended." Let's condense this: in a trance you may not be able to function freely.

Here is the second Secret:
Darkest Secret #2:
Manipulators Put You into a Trance.

To protect yourself, you must learn to use Countermeasures to Break the Trance.

All the Countermeasures (actions you can take to break the trance) in this book will make you stronger and more capable of protecting yourself.

Now, we'll view the third Secret:
Darkest Secret #3:
Manipulators Care Nothing for You and Human Decency: They'll lie, cheat, and do whatever they need to do so they win—but their charm masks all this.

Let's return to the example of a Manipulator selling you a house. A Manipulator does not pause for an instant to see if you can truly afford the new house. The Manipulator would neglect to mention that you will not only have your mortgage payment of $900. There will be additional costs: home repairs, property tax, water, electricity, homeowner's insurance, and more. The Manipulator only emphasizes what he or she knows you want to hear: "Look! $900 is better than the $1500 you're paying for rent, which is just going down the toilet. And the $900 is an investment."

Let's go back to **Darkest Secret #1:**
Manipulators make you hurt and then offer the salve.

The Manipulator has you feeling good about the solution (salve) and feeling bad about your current life situation.

How? A Manipulator will make you hurt through questions such as:

- What bothers you about paying $1500 a month for rent? (The Manipulator will use a derisive tone when he says the word *rent*.)
- What is *not* smart about paying rent on someone else's house instead of investing in your own house?
- How do you feel about your children walking in the neighborhood where you live now?

Do you see how these questions are designed to make you hurt enough so that you'll buy?

An interviewer asked me, "Tom, aren't these good arguments for purchasing a house?"

"What we're looking at is the *intention* of the influencer," I replied. "Let's look at our definition of a manipulator as one who deviously influences someone with no concern about that person's well-being, and who causes harm to that person. If the person truly cannot afford the house, he or she will be harmed by buying it. If the manipulator conceals the truth, the manipulator is doing harm. That's the important difference."

Some friends of mine are ethical and helpful real estate agents who truthfully reveal the whole situation and help the purchaser achieve her own goals.

In this book, we are talking about another type of person; that is, unethical Manipulators.

* * *

In any given moment, we need to remember the tactics Manipulators use. We will focus on the word D.A.R.K. so you can remember details easily and protect yourself from Manipulators.

D — Dangle something for nothing

A — Alert to scarcity

R — Reveal the Desperate Hot Button
K — Keep on pushing buttons

1. Dangle Something for Nothing

What do conmen and conwomen do to seize your attention? They make you think you're getting a "steal."

I recently saw a documentary in which a conman on a street in England showed a toy that looked like it was dancing. This fake product was actually dancing because of a hidden, invisible thread. The conman was dangling something for nothing. The Entranced Buyer thought he was getting something worth $20 for only $5. That was the trick. The Entranced Buyer felt that he was getting $15 extra of value for his $5. What the Buyer really got was something worth nothing. Similarly, I know someone who purchased a copy of a Disney movie from a street vendor in San Francisco. She brought the copy home and it was unwatchable—and the street vendor was never seen again.

An old phrase goes, "A conman cannot con someone who is not looking for something for nothing."

How to Protect Yourself from "Dangle Something for Nothing"

Stop! Get on your cell phone and talk through the "deal" with someone you know who thinks clearly. Go home. Think about it. Do some research on the Internet. Listen to your gut feelings. If the salesman or conman is too insistent, get away from that Manipulator. Get quiet. Have a cup of water. Cool down. Break the Trance!

Break the Trance and Identify the Crucial Detail

Earlier, I mentioned that a Manipulator puts you into a

trance. An added problem is that we put ourselves into a trance. For example, as you read this, are you thinking about your right toe? Most likely not (unless you stubbed your toe recently). The point is that we only focus on a tiny percentage of what is going on in our life.

Around fifteen years ago, I caused myself trouble because I put myself into a trance. I discovered that under certain conditions, friendship can make you nearly deaf. Here's how: I was producing a song for a motion picture. A good friend was singing backup in the chorus. Because of our friendship, I wanted him to sound great. I completely missed the Crucial Detail. In this kind of situation, the Crucial Detail is that what truly counts is how the lead singer sounds! I made a song that I could not release. What a waste of time and money! I had put myself into a trance.

In any situation in which the Manipulator is "dangling something for nothing," we often fall into a trance and miss the Crucial Detail. The most important detail is *not* that we're saving money if we order before midnight tonight. What counts is whether the product creates a lasting, crucial benefit in our lives. And is the benefit of the product worth the cost? Some people even program themselves to make mistakes by saying, "I can't pass up a bargain." The bargain is *not* the Crucial Detail.

Secrets to Break the Trance

This is the process of B.R.E.A.K.S. It will help you remember the proven methods to break a trance.

B — Breathe
R — Relax
E — Envision

A — Act on aromas
K — Keep moving
S — Smile

Secret #1: Breathe

Remember Secret #1: Manipulators make you hurt and then offer the salve. The Manipulator wants to put you into a state of being that fills you with a sense of urgency and anxiety. Oh, no! I'm going to miss the sale!

Stop this highly vulnerable state. Take a deep breath. Do it now. Take a deep breath and let your belly "get fat" by filling it with air. As you breathe out, let your belly deflate. Breathe in through your nose and breathe out through your mouth. This is called belly-breathing. Repeat the actions of belly-breathing three times. Good. Now, do you feel different? Remember, when you are relaxed, you are strong.

Secret #2: Relax

You become stronger when you condition yourself to relax in the face of adversity. Researchers note that when an Olympic athlete is confronted with the most stressful moment in her life, she has prepared in advance. She has given herself ways to calm down. Two powerful methods are described in this section about B.R.E.A.K.S. One is breathing, and the other is envisioning.

A special part of relaxing is the effective use of your posture. Many of us think that we're relaxed when we slouch. However, I was taught by three physical therapists that when you sit up and align your vertebrae, you are more relaxed because your back's bone structure is naturally supporting you. Many of us discover that placing a pillow behind the lumbar-area of our back helps us sit up better. If you are sitting or standing when talking with a Manipulator, ensure that your posture is aligned. You will have more power to protect yourself.

Secret #3: Envision

Envision an image that makes you feel strong. Often, our strongest images come from movies that we saw when we were young. Some of my clients envision being strong like Xena the Warrior Princess or Superman. One client thinks of Sean Connery as James Bond. Immediately, this client walks smoothly with poise. He feels confident. Act as if you are, and you are!

Also, envision yourself being quite aware of your surroundings. On vacation, many of us become entranced by our new surroundings. Travelers let their guard down. A conperson catches them at a weak moment. It's important to stay in the present and be alert to what's going on. Stay present with your needs, and shop around before making a large purchase. Be prepared to walk away.

Watch out for Manipulators who are slick, fast talkers. They try to get your money, and just minutes after they succeed, you realize what happened.

But this is *not* for you! You can remind yourself with an internal comment: "I am aware. What is really going on here?"

Secret #4: Act on Aromas

Let's notice the power of an aroma.

Smell is a potent wizard that transports you across thousands of miles and all the years you have lived. – Helen Keller

Nothing is more memorable than a smell. One scent can be unexpected, momentary and fleeting, yet conjure up a childhood

summer beside a lake in the mountains. – Diane Ackerman

You need to be able to calm down within seconds. One of the fastest ways to do that is to use a favorite aroma. One of my clients has conditioned herself to calm down by smelling lavender. The process for her was to recline in a hot bath and smell lavender simultaneously. Now, the smell of lavender relaxes her limbs quickly.

Remember, when you are relaxed, you neutralize the Manipulator's tactic to make you feel that buying something now is an urgent matter. You let go of any anxious feelings the Manipulator seeks to create in you. Use an aroma to help you feel relaxed and strong.

Secret #5: Keep Moving

A trance often transfixes or freezes us, making us still. Sometimes, the most powerful way to break a trance is to use a movement that you prepared in advance. One of my clients closes his right fist and taps it on his right thigh. In his mind, he repeats the phrase: "I am my own person!" This helps him break out of a trance induced by a Manipulator.

Another client quietly snaps her fingers near her waist. This reminds her to "snap out of it."

Excerpt from
Darkest Secrets of Persuasion and Seduction Masters: How to Protect Yourself and Turn the Power to Good

Purchase your copy of this book (paperback or ebook) at Amazon.com or BarnesandNoble.com
See **Free Chapters** of Tom Marcoux's 32 books at http://amzn.to/ZiCTRj

ABOUT THE AUTHOR

You want more and better, right? Imagine fulfilling your Big Dream.

Tom Marcoux can help you—in that he's coached thousands of people: CEOs, small business leaders, graduate students (at Stanford University) speakers, and authors.

Marcoux is known as an effective **Executive Coach** and **Spoken Word Strategist.**

(and Thought Leader—okay, writing 32 books helped with that!)

** *CEOs, Vice-Presidents, Other Executives, Small Business Leaders:*

You know that leading people and speaking at your best can be tough.

Marcoux solves problems while helping you amplify your own Charisma, Confidence and Control of Time.

Interested? Email Marcoux—tomsupercoach@gmail.com

Ask for a *Special Report:*

* 9 Deadly Mistakes to Avoid for Your Next Speech

** *Speakers, Experts—for a great TED Talk, Book, Audio Book, Speeches, YouTube Videos.*

Marcoux solves problems while helping you to make your Concise, Compelling Message that gets people to trust you and get what you're offering (product, service, *an idea*).

Yes—the *San Francisco Examiner* designated Tom Marcoux as "The Personal Branding Instructor." Marcoux is a professional member of the National Speakers Association for 15 years.

Marcoux is an expert on STORY. He won a Special Award

at the EMMY AWARDS, and he directed a feature film that went to the CANNES FILM MARKET and earned international distribution.

(Marcoux helps you *Be Heard and Be Trusted* . . . that's his 15th Anniversary, 3rd edition book.)

As a CEO, Marcoux leads teams in the United Kingdom, India and the USA. Marcoux guides clients & audiences (IBM, Sun Microsystems, etc.) in leadership, team-building, power time management and branding. See Tom's Popular BLOG: www.TomSuperCoach.com

Specialties: coach to CEOS * Executives * Small Business Owners * Leaders * Speakers * Experts * Authors * Academics

One of his *Darkest Secrets* books rose to #1 on Amazon.com Hot New Releases in Business Life (and in Business Communication). Marcoux is a Executive Coach and guest expert on TV, radio, and print.

Marcoux addressed the National Association of Broadcasters' Conference six years running. With a degree in psychology, Tom is a guest lecturer at **Stanford University**, DeAnza College & California State University, and teaches business communication, designing careers, public speaking, science fiction cinema/literature and comparative religion at Academy of Art University. He is engaged in book/film projects *Crystal Pegasus* (children's) and *Jack AngelSword* (thriller-fantasy). See Tom's well-received blogs

at www.BeHeardandBeTrusted.com

at www.YourBodySoulandProsperity.com

Consider engaging **Tom Marcoux as your Executive Coach.**

"As Tom's client for many years, I have benefited from his wisdom and strategic approach. Do your career and personal life a big favor and get his books and engage him as **your Executive Coach**." – Dr. JoAnn Dahlkoetter, author of *Your Performing Edge* and Coach to CEOs and Olympic Gold Medalists

"**Tom Marcoux coached me to get more done in 10 days than other coaches in 2 years.**" – Brad Carlson, CEO of MindStrong LLC

Tom Marcoux can help you with **speech writing** and **coaching for your best performance.**
As Tom says, *Make Your Speech a Pleasant Beach.*
Join Tom's Linkedin.com group: *Executive Public Speaking and Communication Power.*
At Google+: join the community "Create Your Best Life – Charisma & Confidence"
Get a **Free** report: "9 Deadly Mistakes to Avoid for Your Next Speech and 9 Surefire Methods" at
http://tomsupercoach.com/freereport9Mistakes4Speech.html

Tom Marcoux has trained CEOs, small business owners, and graduate students to speak with impact and gain audiences' tremendous approval and cooperation. *Learn how to present and get thunderous applause!*
"Tom, Thanks for your coaching and work with me on revising my speech at a major university. Working with you has been so enlightening for me. Through your gentle prodding and guidance I was able to write a speech that connects with the audience. I wish everyone could experience the transformation I have undergone. You have helped me discover the warm and compelling stories that now make my speech reach hearts and uplift minds. This was truly an empowering experience. I cannot thank you enough for your great assistance." — J.S.

"Tom Marcoux has been an NAB Conference favorite [speaker] for six years. And he is very energetic."
– John Marino, Vice President, National Association of Broadcasters, Washington, D.C.

"Using just one of Tom Marcoux's methods, I got more done in 2 weeks than in 6 months."
– Jaclyn Freitas, M.A.

Tom's Coaching features innovations:
- Dynamic Rehearsal
- Power Rehearsal for Crisis
- The Charisma Advantage that Saves You Time

Become a fan of Tom's graphic novels/feature films:
- Fantasy Thriller: *Jack AngelSword*
  type "JackAngelSword" at Facebook.com
- Science fiction: *TimePulse*
  www.facebook.com/timepulsegraphicnovel
- Children's Fantasy: *Crystal Pegasus*
  www.facebook.com/crystalpegasusandrose
- Young Adult Fantasy: *Jenalee Storm*
  At Facebook.com "Jenalee Storm."

See **Free Chapters** of Tom Marcoux's 32 books at http://amzn.to/ZiCTRj   Amazon.com

Your Notes:

Your Notes:

_____

_____

_____

_____

_____

_____

_____

Area for Your Sketches of Your Ideas:

www.ingramcontent.com/pod-product-compliance
Lightning Source LLC
Chambersburg PA
CBHW070457100426
42743CB00010B/1655